PHILOSOPHY IN AMERICA
AN AMS REPRINT SERIES

JONATHAN EDWARDS

AMS PRESS
NEW YORK

Jonathan Edwards.

𝕮𝖗𝖊𝖆𝖙𝖎𝖛𝖊 𝕷𝖎𝖛𝖊𝖘

~~~~~~

Jonathan Edwards

by

ARTHUR CUSHMAN MCGIFFERT, JR.
*Professor of Christian Theology in
the Chicago Theological
Seminary*

1932
HARPER & BROTHERS PUBLISHERS
New York and London

Library of Congress Cataloging in Publication Data

McGiffert, Arthur Cushman, 1892–
  Jonathan Edwards.

  (Philosophy in America)
  Reprint of the 1st ed. published by Harper, New York,
in series: Creative lives.
  Bibliography: p.
  Includes index.
  1. Edwards, Jonathan, 1703–1758.   I. Title.
II. Series.
BX7260.E3M4   1980   285.8′092′4   75-3134
ISBN 0-404-59143-4

Reprinted by arrangement with
Harper & Row, Publishers, Inc.

Reprinted from the edition of 1932, New York. Trim size and text
area of the original have been slightly altered. [original trim size:
13.2 × 20 cm; text area: 8.4 × 15.2 cm].

MANUFACTURED
IN THE UNITED STATES OF AMERICA

To

A. C. M.

πατρὶ καὶ διδασκάλῳ

Contents

I. AT YALE	1
II. CHOOSING A CAREER	14
III. RELIGION COME ALIVE	37
IV. RELIGION UNDER THE MICROSCOPE	68
V. PLAY AND WORK	90
VI. THE SACRED GADFLY OF NORTHAMPTON	109
VII. EXILE	139
VIII. HIDDEN RIVERS	165
IX. MINDS ACROSS THE SEA	186
X. AT PRINCETON	201
ACKNOWLEDGMENTS	215
BOOKS TO CONSULT	217
CHRONOLOGY	221
INDEX	223

Jonathan Edwards

Chapter One

AT YALE

In Colonial America at the close of the seventeenth century the temperature of religion was an even moderate warmth. The passion which had thrust the Colonists on to the Atlantic coastal plain and spurred them into the hill country beyond was spent. A second and third generation were taking life more tranquilly. But the undying flame of religion burst forth again in ardor of devotion and flash of aspiration, setting the age afire. In one frail figure, a native American, the elemental spark again became gloriously incandescent, destructive of old complacencies, generative of vital convictions and luminous with fresh insights.

At the time of Jonathan Edwards' birth, October 5, 1703, his father was minister in Windsor, the earliest settlement in Connecticut, a rural community with little to lift it above the commonplace of its frontier environment. Timothy Edwards, Jonathan's father, of well-to-do merchant stock of Hartford, had been graduated from Harvard in 1691 and was the first student ever to receive both the Bachelor of Arts and the Master of Arts degrees on the same day. The social position of his family, however, was such that he was placed last in the list of the graduating class, in keeping with the then Harvard custom of arranging the names of students not alphabetically, but according to the prestige or social rank of the family. For sixty-three years he ministered to his parish on the east side of "Ye Great River," a studious, thoughtful man and a forceful preacher, but handicapped by uncongenial agricultural responsibilities, for he possessed a large farm, the gift of his father, which with the help of a slave he had to work to eke out his salary.

His other source of extra-professional income was private tutoring, a common avocation of the New England minister. Through Timothy Edwards' hands passed many of the boys of Windsor to prepare for college. There still exist his bills for the tutoring of Wolcotts and Stoughtons and Stiles and others who were later to assume positions of leadership in the government, judiciary, and ministry of the state.

Timothy Edwards also taught his own children. He must have been a "born teacher" and much in advance of his time in his educational theories, to have given each of his ten girls the equivalent of a college-preparatory course. At this time most New England girls had to be content if they learned to read and write. Timothy Edwards even managed to send his daughters to a kind of finishing-school in Boston, where his wife, the daughter of the noted Solomon Stoddard, minister of Northampton, had in her girlhood received "a su-

AT YALE

perior education." Later, when his daughters had all grown up into tall young women, taking after their mother in this respect, their father used to refer to them with affectionate jocosity and pride as his "sixty feet of daughters."

Young Jonathan, the only son, had his lessons in the same room with his four older sisters. Each child went ahead as fast as inclination and ability dictated. When the parent-teacher was called away to serve as chaplain with the expedition against Canada, he wrote back to his wife that Jonathan was to continue to recite his Latin with one of his older sisters, adding that he had "left paper enough for them which they may use to that end, only I would have you reserve enough for your own use in writing letters, etc." That the boy was no prig or plaster saint, for all his brains, is clear from a further passage in the letter: "I hope thou wilt take special care of Jonathan that he dont learn to be rude and naught, etc.—of which thou and I have lately discoursed." Jonathan was then nearly eight. He had begun to study Latin when he was six. Obviously his father's educational program involved no waste of intellectual effort. Small wonder that Jonathan went to college with a reading knowledge of Latin, Greek, and Hebrew, and with a developed interest in natural science which his father had been at pains to cultivate. The boy came to appreciate his early training. Looking back upon his parents' home-made education from the sudden perspective of his early twenties, he jotted down in his Journal: "I have great reason to believe that their counsel and education have been my making; though, in the time of it, it seemed to do me so little good."

When, in 1716, Edwards entered the collegiate school of Connecticut it had not yet received from Governor Elihu Yale of London the large box of books, the picture and arms of King George, and the English textiles, all to the value of £800, which prompted the trustees solemnly to name the college after him. Of Edwards' participation in social and other non-academic activities during his college career little is known. His Journal intimates that he had few friends in college. As a matter of fact, he was deficient in good-nature. There was nothing happy-go-lucky about him. He was impatient of stupidity and sharp-tongued, critical and altogether too ready to laugh at the faults and infirmities of his fellow-students, expressing his scorn of laziness and time-wasting. He could not take people as he found them, but must always try to improve them. He was essentially a student and preoccupied with an inner world of ambitions and moods.

At the beginning of his senior year the trustees appointed the seventeen-year-old Edwards to the position of butler, an office ordinarily reserved for a graduate student. The youth who was to become America's leading theologian and secure for his country its first measure of intellectual prestige abroad was selected to serve bread and beer at the student commons and to check up on the broken windows and other damages caused by the students in the dormitory. What country, other than America, could furnish so engaging a spectacle! To be sure, the trustees' vote indicated some intelligent misgivings on their part as to Edwards' interest and fitness and provided for the selection of an alternate butler in case he should decline the appointment.

For the first two decades of its history Yale had been divided into three parts. Some of the students and the library were still at Saybrook, the original site of the college; others, Edwards among them, with one of the best tutors, were at Weathersfield; the remainder, at New Haven. These communities were bidding against one another for the permanent location of the college. The trustees finally voted in favor of New Haven, but it took an act of the General Court to induce the students from upriver to come down to the seacoast. Student strikes were not infrequent at the time. The Weathersfield boys had not been in New Haven two months when, on January 10, 1719, they "mutinied" and returned to Weathersfield. "Mr. Johnson," Edwards wrote his sister, "was the cause of our coming away." This "Mr. Johnson" became in due time the founder and first president of King's College, in New York City, now known as Columbia University. His insufficiency of learning was the alleged reason of the students' strike. But though they removed the tutor, the trustees asserted that Johnson was a gentleman of sufficient learning, and spread on the minutes a vote of particular thanks and ordered that three pounds be paid him for his "extraordinary service." Samuel Johnson may have been the innocent victim of local political rivalry. On the other hand, in his own account of the incident, he remarked that "he was always both by himself and his friends designed for the pulpit." Perhaps he really was not a good teacher and suffered by comparison with the brilliant tutor of Weathersfield, Elisha Williams, who was to shine like an evil star in Edwards' life. Three years later Johnson, as well as the rector and tutors of Yale College, caused a scandal of major importance in Connecticut by leaving the Church of their fathers and going over to the Church of England. Johnson, Benjamin Franklin and Jonathan Edwards were the leading intellectual figures of eighteenth-century America.

Narrow as was the curriculum of Yale when Edwards entered, meager as were its resources in books, in equipment, and in the choice of instructors, the boy's alert mind leaped into furious activity at college.

According to its charter of 1701 Yale was founded for the instruction of youth in the arts and sciences in preparation for "public employment both in Church and Civil State." The board of trustees, however, seem to have been interested primarily in the training of ministers and in their initial meeting set up a curriculum that should "promote the power and Purity of Religion and Best Edification and peace of these New England churches." The course of studies they arranged was to include "theoretical divinity" and homiletics. Students were to be required to learn by heart "the Assemblies Catechism in Latin and Ames's Theological Theses of which as Also Ames's Cases, the Rector shall make or Cause to be made from time to time such Explanations as may be (through the Blessing of God) most Conducive to their Establishment in the Principles of the Christian protestant religion." As for homiletics, the rector, following the practice at Harvard, was to "Expound practical Theology or Cause the students non Graduated to Repeat Sermons."

Courses in Cicero and Virgil were also required, as well as the New Testament in Greek and the Hebrew Psalter. From a letter Edwards sent home at the end of his junior year we learn of other studies. He asked his father to get him "Alstead's Geometry and Gassendus' Astronomy; with which I would intreat you to get a pair of dividers or mathematician's compasses, and a scale, which are absolutely necessary in order to learning mathematics; and also, the *Art of Thinking*."

Edwards was likewise reading the third Earl of Shaftesbury's treatises on ethics and studying science. But far more important than anything yet mentioned was John Locke's *Essay on the Human Understanding*. It was one of the volumes included in the Dummer gift to the Yale Library in 1714. Samuel Johnson, the tutor already mentioned, seems to have been among the first to recognize the significance of the new acquisition and, according to his autobiography, he and the other tutor "introduced the studies of Mr. Locke and Sir Isaac Newton as fast as they could." They met with opposition in certain quarters and were "cautioned against thinking anything of these authors because the new philosophy, it was said, would soon bring in a new divinity and corrupt the pure religion of the country."

Whether Edwards was introduced to Locke directly by Johnson or not, he flamed into an equal enthusiasm for the radical English philosopher, finding in him, as he said, "a far higher pleasure than the most greedy miser finds, when gathering up handfuls of silver and gold, from some newly discovered treasure." Locke's psychological insight, his critical attitude, his insistence on subjecting to fresh examination the constitution and operations of the human mind, not only enriched Edwards' thinking, but fired him to independent investigations for himself. In his excitement he characteristically filled page after page of his college notebooks with reflections prompted by his reading of this epoch-making book. Edwards thought with his pen in his hand—a habit learned at home—ever ready to jot down ideas that came to him in the course of his reading and occasionally resorting to shorthand when his ideas jostled one another too rapidly or some notion occurred to him that he was not of a mind to have any eye but his own see.

Work in the class-room did not exhaust his intellectual efforts. Before he had been long in college he began to fancy himself an author with an international public, and to put down on paper the outlines of projected books. It took a bold and comprehensive imagination and a reach that was unafraid of exceeding its grasp, for a fifteen-year-old boy to propose: "TITLE. The Natural History of the Mental World or of the Internal World: being a Particular Enquiry into the Nature of the Human Mind with respect to both its faculties—the Understanding and the Will—and its various Instincts and Active and Passive Powers." Even more remarkable is the fact that in the outline immediately following of "subjects to be handled in the Treatise on the Mind" almost every important problem he later dealt with is noted down, often with a prophetic hint of his solution. His intellectual life thereafter was to be devoted not to the raising of new problems, but to the solution of problems already anticipated.

Edwards was well aware how presumptuous and childish his ambitions would appear to the outsider. So he wrote down the most grandiose of them in his home-made, unpunctuated shorthand which patient and painstaking study has partially deciphered. "Before I venture to publish in London to make some experiment in my own country, to play at small games first. That I may gain some experience in writing, first to write letters to some in England and to try my hand in lesser matters before I venture in great." His mind was forging ahead into fresh and unfamiliar fields. "This has been thought of before," is his note appended to one of his early reflections. But already germinating in his fertile mind were other less familiar ideas, which he foresaw would make headway only against opposition:

Bring in those things that are very much out of the way of the World's thinking as little as possible in the beginning of a treatise. It wont do for it will give an ill-prejudice a tincture to the reader's mind in reading the rest. Let them have a good opinion by beginning with the other first and then they will more easily receive strange things from me. If I tell it at first, it will look something like affectation of telling something strange to the world.

Edwards was conscious of another handicap besides that of his youthfulness, a handicap peculiar to his time. "The world," he said, and the word itself reveals his far-reaching objectives, "will expect more modesty because of my circumstances in America." He shared to the end of his life the feeling of inferiority under which intellectual America suffered at this time.

His future success as a writer might be prophesied on the basis of the general rules he set down for authorship. A selected few will serve to indicate the early development of his craftmanship:

1. Try not only to silence but to gain. . . .

3. What is prefatorial, not to write in a distinct preface or introduction but in the body of the work. Then I shall be sure to have it read by every one. . . . [The tribe of "short-cut" reviewers of books had evidently not come into prominence in Edwards' day.]

7. When I would prove anything to take special care that the matter be so stated that it shall be seen

most Clearly and Distinctly by everyone just how much I would prove; and to Extricate all Questions from the least confusion or ambiguity of words so that the Ideas shall be left naked.

8. In the course of Reasoning not to Pretend anything to be more certain than Every one will Plainly see it is, by such expressions as its certain, its undeniable, etc. . . .

11. Never to dispute for things after that I cannot handsomely Retreat upon conviction of the contrary.

In addition to this scrutiny of literary techniques and the decision in favor of modesty, accuracy, and clarity of presentation Edwards scrutinized himself and undertook while in college a discipline far more difficult than the discipline of style. He recognized and accepted responsibility for the direction of his life. He would be no drifter, unaware of the forces operating within and about him. He would try to see himself as he really was, without the whitewash of ignorance and self-deceit. Before ever psychologists had invented the term "rationalization" he had "concluded to endeavor to work myself into duties by searching and tracing back all the real reasons why I do not do them and narrowly searching out all the subtle subterfuges of my thoughts and answering them to the utmost of my power." So eager was he to understand himself that he turned for illumination to the subconscious workings of his mind. "I think it a very good way to examine dreams every morning when I awake; what are the nature, circumstances, principles and ends of my imaginary actions and passions in them;

in order to discern what are my prevailing inclinations, etc." His introspectiveness reveals his profound psychological interest. But he did not stop short with analysis. Deliberately he set about to temper his character into steel. Not uncommonly do young people write down resolutions in their diaries, but not always are they as searchingly specific and revealing as the seventy Edwards jotted down at one time and another before he reached his majority. His Journal shows him inventing a kind of measurement test for character development: "This week the weekly account rose higher than ordinary. . . . Sabbath day, Jan. 20. At night. I fell exceedingly low in the weekly account."

He began to experiment with himself, observing the results of these experiments in self-discipline with careful objectivity. One Saturday night he confided to his Journal, "The last Wednesday took up a resolution to refrain from all manner of evil speaking for one week, to try it and see the effect of it," adding that already he found the effect of it such that he could not but take for granted that it was "a duty to be observed for ever." Finding himself habitually impatient at the church meeting, he took steps to change his attitude and was able to report to himself that he had been so far successful in his striving that there was "a prospect of making church attendance easy and delightful and very profitable in time." The outcome of one curious device for escaping from temptation by doing "some sum in Arithmetic or

Geometry or some other study which necessarily engages all my thoughts and unavoidably keeps them from wandering" he unfortunately did not describe. Some one suggested that he was overdoing his ascetic practice of fasting; it would be prejudicial to his health. To this he replied that he would plainly feel it and experience it before he ceased. After further trial he noted in the Journal, "Again confirmed by experience of the happy effects of a strict temperance with respect both to body and mind." "I think I find myself more sprightly and healthy both in body and mind for my self-denial in eating, drinking and sleeping." Sprightliness is hardly the adjective a biographer would think of applying to Edwards. But he possessed a brilliant intellect and a steady thrust of will.

Mind and character thus disciplined, Edwards was ready for productive work at an age when most of his contemporaries and most college men today are still engaged in horseplay and extra-curricular activities. What should he do?

Chapter Two

CHOOSING A CAREER

1. SCIENCE?

A boy with one talent finds the choice of a career fairly simple. To the boy with no particular talent or with many talents the difficulty of choice is multiplied and his final decision regarding a career often poignantly delayed.

Edwards had many talents. The earliest to develop was an intense interest in natural science. Among the extant manuscripts of his boyhood are accounts of spiders and of rainbows that, oddly enough, prove extraordinarily prophetic of certain phases of his later development.

And this, Sir, is the way of spiders Going from one tree to Another at a great distance and this is the way of their flying in the Air and altho I say I am Certain of it, I Dont Desire that the truth of it should be Received upon my word tho I Could bring others to testify to it to whom I have shewn it and who have looked on with admiration to see their Manner of Working but every ones eyes that will take the Pains to Observe will make them as sure of it: Only those that would make Experiment must take notice that it is not Every sort of Spider that is a flying Spider for those spiders that keep in houses are of a quite

Different sort, as also those that keep in the Ground and those that keep in swamps, in hollow trees and Rotten logs; but those spiders that keep on branches of trees and shrubs are the flying spiders, they delight most in walnut trees, and are that sort of spiders that make those Curious net work polygonal webs that are so frequently to be seen in the Latter End of the year.

Edwards was ten or twelve when he wrote out these careful and detailed observations. They show him already possessed of a painstaking and discriminating intellect. He dealt with facts at first hand and with the patience and persistence of a John Muir or a Jean Henri Fabre. He trusted the correctness of his own findings, but at the same time was ready to submit them to the testing of another observer. He was ingenious in developing experiments and hypotheses to explain obscure phenomena.

This same account of the habits of the flying spider exhibits still another characteristic feature of his mind.

Standing at Some Distance behind the End of an house or some other Opake body so as just to hide the Disk of the sun and keep off his Dazling Rays, and looking along Close by the side of it, I have seen vast multitudes of little shining webs and Glistening strings brightly reflecting the Sunbeams and some of them of Great length and of such a height that One would think they were tacked to the vault of the heavens and would be burnt like tow in the Sun. And make a very beautiful, pleasing, as well as surprizing Appearance.

Edwards was evidently more than a keen observer. He had an eye for nature's loveliness as well as for its facts. Astonishing as was his capacity for observation, his power of appreciation kept pace with it. Detached he could be and analytical in recording what his eyes reported to him, fresh and untrammeled by tradition in his first-hand acquaintance with the actual behaviors and characteristics of the world of nature. But his eye was also fresh and sensitive to loveliness, to "beauties of nature in the air and on the face of the earth," as he was to put it later. A relentless curiosity was the root of his devotion to science. A love of beauty made him an artist. These two approaches to the world were permanent highways along which his mind constantly traveled.

Edwards carried with him to college his youthful enthusiasm for natural science. There he soaked himself in the subject. His free-ranging intellect and his growing knowledge combined to open up many an alluring new topic for investigation. He crammed his notebook with interrogations. "Why, having two eyes, do we not see double?" "To show, from Sir Isaac Newton's principles of light and colors, why the sky is blue; why the Sun is yellow when rising and setting, and sometimes in smoky weather of a blood red; why Distant Mountains are blue, etc." Most striking of all the "things to be considered or written fully about" in the realm of physics is stated thus: "To observe, that all rays of one sort, being obstructed by any medium, and others still proceeding, as by the air in smoky weather, etc.:—to enquire how it can be, and to observe that its so doing makes it probable that there are some other properties in light and also mediums yet wholly unknown . . . and to enquire what it is and also to seek out other strange phenomena and compare them altogether and see what quality can be made out of them: and if we can discover them it is probable we may be let into a New World of Philosophy." Edwards felt himself trembling on the brink of the discovery of a new physical theory.

His curiosity was constantly on tiptoe. The commonest experience would start his mind in pursuit of an explanation; as for example, his noticing the color of the sunlight shining on the page of his book through the leaves of the tree under which he sat reading. Why was it of a reddish-purplish color?

Many departments of scientific knowledge attracted his interest. Botany, for instance, and physiology and geology: "to observe about all the mountains being pitched over to the westward." But oftenest his mind was preoccupied with problems in the field of astronomical physics: "to know the shape of the Spheroid of the Universe by observation of the milky way, and to know whereabouts our system is in it. . . . To show that the Starry World cannot be infinite because it is a Spheroid."

Edwards might have made a great name for

himself in natural science had he not been born a century too soon. In his day American science was in its infancy. Such research as there was—the names of Benjamin Franklin and Cadwallader Colden come to mind—was largely avocational. The economic value of science was little recognized. Even after the middle of the century a leading educator of Philadelphia could write to a minister in Newport this rather grudging commendation of his investigations in connection with the comet of 1759: "I am far from blaming you for your careful and accurate researches; it may make you more useful here and form your taste to examine the works of God with a higher satisfaction in the coming world."

Unfavorable conditions closed for Edwards the door to a professional career in entomology or physics, though, as his first biographer reports, he continued to "cultivate his uncommon taste for natural philosophy to the end of his life." He read the *Transactions of the Royal Society* when he could lay hands on them. His reading-list notes one after another of Sir Isaac Newton's books. And to the career he finally did choose he brought a curiosity and an empirical spirit that distinguished him among the religious leaders of America. In the field of the psychology of religion, particularly, his early interests and training were to stand him in good stead. Yet it may be doubted whether Edwards would have become a scientist even had the circumstances been more favorable.

2. From Science to Philosophy

It took a mighty passion to tear Edwards away from the beckoning vistas of scientific research But such a passion burned within him. He yearned for a more difficult knowledge; facts, for all their fascination, could not permanently satisfy him. He wanted to know the meaning of existence. Scientific knowledge seemed to him inadequate on two accounts. It was fragmentary. It dealt with segments of the field of knowledge. It suggested, but never achieved, an all-inclusive system. He wanted comprehensiveness. He could not help "putting and tying things together." He wanted to see life whole. Science was also superficial. If it could answer every question it asked, the human mind would still be dissatisfied. Edwards wanted, as he said, to search into the "innermost nature of things." He turned to philosophy.

According to William Ernest Hocking, "The history of thought has been very largely controlled by the fact that to some men the rock is the impressive and sufficient type of reality, to others the feeling or the 'mind.'" Edwards belonged in the second group. "Things spiritual" were to him the eternal verities. He was hardly out of his boyhood before he came to the conclusion that things are not what they seem. Appearances are deceitful. "Colors are not really in the things, no more than pain is in a needle, but strictly nowhere else but in the mind." "Corporeal things exist no otherwise than mentally." The world is, philosophically speaking, "an ideal one"; that is to say, "the Material Universe is absolutely dependent on the conception of the mind for its existence." The mind on which the universe is thus dependent is not the human mind alone. Human minds have not always existed. That nothing should exist, however, Edwards declared unthinkable; "it is the essence of all contradictions." But it is equally "impossible that the world should exist from Eternity without a Mind." "Hence we learn the necessity of the Eternal Existence of an All-comprehending Mind."

The universe or material world, which exists "nowhere but in the divine mind," is perceived by various human minds in much the same way because of God's establishment of certain laws whereby our minds apprehend his ideas. In so far as our ideas of corporeal things agree with the ideas of God we have arrived at truth. To summarize his position in his own words:

That, which truly is the Substance of all Bodies, is *the infinitely exact and precise and perfectly stable Idea in God's mind, together with his stable Will that the same shall gradually be communicated to us and to other minds, according to certain fixed and exact established Methods and Laws:* or in somewhat different language, *the infinitely exact and precise Divine Idea, together with an answerable, perfectly exact, precise and stable Will, with respect to correspondent communications to Created Minds and effects on their minds.*

The world of sensation and perception has become, on analysis, a shadow world, having no proper being of its own. To illustrate what he meant as well perhaps as to suggest the affinities of his thought, Edwards copied into his notebook Plato's famous myth of the cave, which he quoted from Cudworth's *Intellectual System.*

"Plato, in his *Subterranean Cave,* so famously known and so elegantly described by him, supposes men tied with their backs towards the Light, placed at a great distance from them, so that they could not turn about their heads to it neither, and therefore could see nothing but the shadows of certain substances behind them, projected from it; which shadows they concluded to be the only substance and realities. And when they heard the sounds made by those bodies that were betwixt the Light and them, or their reverberated echoes, they imputed them to those shadows which they saw. All this is a description of the state of those men who take Body to be the only Real and Substantial Thing in the world, and to do all that is done in it; and therefore often impute Sense, Reason and Understanding, to nothing but Blood and Brains in us."

Historians of thought have been at some pains to discover the sources of Edwards' idealistic metaphysics. Locke undoubtedly set him thinking, but Locke did not supply him with his conclusions. The Irish bishop, George Berkeley, fountain-head of so much of modern idealism, was for many years believed to have had in Edwards his first American follower. But that honor belongs rather to the Samuel Johnson already mentioned, who became not only Berkeley's disciple, but also his personal friend during the bishop's stay in Rhode Island in connection with the campaign for a missionary college in Bermuda. Edwards could not have been acquainted with Berkeley's writings when he formulated his own philosophy.

A more plausible source of his ideas is Ralph Cudworth. A century later Ralph Waldo Emerson was to read the inchoate and tedious pages of this Cambridge Platonist and have his mind set into a ferment by their yeasty Platonic elements. But attractive as this suggestion is, the sole evidence of Edwards' early acquaintance with Cudworth is this quotation, which he may have picked up at second-hand.

As a matter of fact, the attempt to trace the sources of Edwards' ideas may be wholly beside the point. His theories may well have had no specific paternity. There are not many ways in which the human mind can interpret its experience. Types of philosophy are relatively few in number. It is quite possible that the brilliant young Edwards spontaneously originated his idealistic philosophy.

His reflections led him to perceive difficulties lurking in his interpretation of existence as fundamentally mental. In part they were due to loose definitions: "When we say that the World, i. e. the material Universe, exists nowhere but in the mind we have got to such a degree of strictness and abstraction that we must be exceedingly careful that we do not confound and lose ourselves by misapprehension." The idealist must also constantly struggle against the prejudices arising from appearances. "The World seems so differently to our eyes, to our ears and other senses, from the idea we have of it by Reason, that we can hardly realize the latter." Spirits seem more like shadows and material things more substantial, though the reverse is true. The trouble is that our imaginations are at fault. When we stop to think, however, we recognize how real are "thought, inclination or delight," though they have not three dimensions. To see the absurdity of any other interpretation we have only to ask: "How large is that thing in the Mind which they call Thought? Is Love square or round? Is the surface of hatred rough or smooth? Is Joy an inch, or a foot, in diameter?"

Other difficulties in his theory arose, as he acknowledged, from the fact that it seems to make no practical difference in life. His principles, for instance, do not "at all make void Natural Philosophy or the Science of the Causes or Reasons of Corporeal changes." Science seeks to understand "the proportion of God's acting; and the case is the same as to such proportions, whether we suppose the World only mental in our sense, or no." The plain man, too, may pursue his affairs without perplexing his mind with a thousand questions and doubts.

In the realm of ethics, however, he insisted that his theory made a profound difference. Metaphysical and ethical idealism have always been near-cousins. Each of them resolves an apparent dualism of experience. The vividness of Edwards' experience of the dualism between impulse and ideal has already been described. He was content with no solution short of the victory of the ideal. "No happiness is solid and substantial but spiritual happiness, though it may seem that sensual pleasures are more real and spiritual only imaginary; just as it seems as if sensible matter were only real and spiritual substance only imaginary." His idealistic metaphysics validated his intuition as to the kinds of things which he took to be real. It met the rational necessities of thought by unifying and systematizing the data of existence in the unity of the Divine Mind. It interpreted his moral experience. His metaphysics supported his ethics and was in turn invigorated by his ethics.

3. From Philosophy to Theology

At the present time a man with Edwards' philosophical interests is likely to choose college teaching as the career which will give him the best opportunity to carry on his reflective life. In his day there were no laymen on the college faculties. Ecclesiastical ordination was the only gateway into the teaching profession.

Edwards' shift from philosophy to theology may perhaps be most easily explained in the light of this situation. Whether primarily interested in theology or not, he must study it if he wanted to be able to pursue his philosophical speculations. His decision in favor of the ministry may have been due to his intellectual interests. Yet such an explanation is too simple to be wholly adequate. The academic mind sometimes imagines that philosophy is indulged in only by those who professionally teach the subject in a university or that it prospers best in the rarefied atmosphere of the classroom. But we are aware that there is likely to be as good philosophy on the farm or in the office as there is on the campus. Edwards, like others of his contemporaries, might have become a philosopher-farmer or a philosopher-physician or a philosopher-man of affairs. Something more than his intellectual ambition decided him against philosophy and in favor of theology.

For one thing, theology is social in its reference and philosophy is individualistic. The philosopher is the lone thinker who works out a theory of life to suit himself and for himself. The theologian works out a theory to suit the church and for the church. The philosopher speaks for himself. The theologian is the interpreter and spokesman for a large and organized group of people with a definite history and program. The very fact that Edwards chose to become a leader in the church is a sign of his deep-seated craving for social reinforcement. That same need of security betrays its presence in the readiness with which on later occasions he sought to bolster up his own thinking by the authority of Scripture. Leadership in the church offered Edwards the two-fold support of a social group and a divine revelation.

The ministry likewise made its appeal to the practical side of his nature. Edwards was not the sort of person who could find permanent satisfaction in pure speculation. Truth for truth's sake did not appeal to him. He was always on the lookout for its "practical improvement." Theology is applied philosophy. It converts truth into life. The theologian's task is to relate the truth as he sees it to the exigencies of daily conduct. This is a task that requires a knowledge of human needs and ambitions. It demands a perpetual attack on the false philosophy that produces erroneous behavior.

Powerful as all these motives were, they could hardly have generated sufficient motive power to induce Edwards to enter the ministry had it not been for his religious experience and temperament. By the time of his graduation from college his religious development was already marked. Taken by itself, his boyhood preoccupation with religious themes and practices might have meant nothing. But in the light of his later development it becomes significantly prophetic. We owe our knowledge of it to an account Edwards wrote when he was nearly forty. Undoubtedly he read back into his earlier experiences some of his later development.

His recorded religious history begins at the time of a revival in his father's church at Windsor. Its effect on the minister's son and his friends was curious. These ten-year-old boys built a "booth" in a swamp for a place of prayer. Edwards does not say how long they used the shack for this purpose. He was also praying in secret and taking much self-righteous pleasure in being pious and "abundant in religious duties." Eventually these youthful "convictions and affections wore off," as well they might.

Another memorable episode was a second revival just before he left home for college. During it his mother and one of his sisters were converted. Edwards himself never had a conventional experience of conversion, a fact which subsequently caused him a good deal of anguish and perplexity. During his college days he passed through a normal period of adolescent doubts, which he attempted to counteract by repeated resolutions and vows to God. Eventually he so far succeeded in his self-discipline—to which reference has already been made—that he "broke off all former wicked ways and all ways of known outward sin." In the light of his later experience he came to the conclusion that neither of these "remarkable seasons of awakening" was a full-fledged religious experience. The ultimate and all-important "change" by which he was brought, as he said, "to those new dispositions and that new sense of things that I have since had" was of another character altogether.

Walter Lippmann has described the discovery that "our wishes have little or no authority in the world" as "the experience of the necessity that is in the nature of things." Edwards recorded his own unforgettable passage from childhood to maturity in Calvinistic rather than in Stoic terms. It occurred in 1721 soon after he left college.

Though he did not recognize it at the time, it was the first phase of his conversion.

> From my childhood up, my mind had been full of objections against the doctrine of God's sovereignty in choosing whom he would to eternal life and rejecting whom he pleased; leaving them eternally to perish and be everlastingly tormented in hell. It used to appear like a very horrible doctrine to me. But I remember the time very well when I seemed to be convinced and fully satisfied as to this sovereignty of God and his justice in thus eternally disposing of men according to his sovereign pleasure. . . . My mind rested in it and it put an end to all those cavils and objections. And there has been a wonderful alteration in my mind with respect to the doctrine of God's sovereignty from that day to this; so that I scarce ever have found so much as the rising of an objection against it, in the most absolute sense, in God's shewing mercy to whom he will shew mercy and hardening whom he will. God's absolute sovereignty and justice with respect to salvation and damnation is what my mind seems to rest assured of as much as any thing that I see with my eyes; at least it is so at times.

Thus Edwards accepted the universe. Seldom thereafter did he falter in his loyalty to this insight of his dawning maturity. It did not at once occur to him to interpret this discovery religiously: "not in the least imagining at the time, nor for a long time after, that there was any extraordinary influence of God's Spirit in it; but only that now I saw further and my reason apprehended the justice and reasonableness of it."

CHOOSING A CAREER

In the meantime, before he had occasion to account for it theologically, the experience itself soon developed a second and less common phase. His acceptance of life did not halt at the stage of a grim Stoicism or an intellectually acceptable Calvinism. "I have often since that first conviction had quite another kind of sense of God's sovereignty than I had then. I have often since had not only a conviction, but a *delightful* conviction. [The italics are his own.] The doctrine has very often appeared exceedingly pleasant, bright and sweet. Absolute sovereignty is what I love to ascribe to God. But my first conviction was not so."

The constant refrain that runs through this autobiographical passage—and it can be duplicated many times in Edwards' writings—is one of eager delight in life.

The first instance that I remember of that sort of inward, sweet delight in God and divine things, that I have lived much in since, was on reading those words, I Tim. 1.17: *Now unto the King eternal, immortal, invisible, the only wise God, be honor and glory, for ever and ever, Amen.* As I read the words there came into my soul and was as it were diffused through it, a sense of the glory of the Divine Being; a new sense, quite different from any thing I had ever experienced before. Never any words of Scripture seemed to me as these words did. I thought with myself how excellent a Being that was and how happy I should be if I might enjoy that God and be rapt up to him in heaven and be as it were swallowed up in him forever! I kept saying and as it were singing over these words of Scripture to myself; and went to pray to God that I might enjoy him and prayed in a manner quite different from what I used to do, with a new sort of affection.

The mystical quality of these emotions comes out even more clearly later in the narrative.

This I know not how to express otherwise than by a calm, sweet abstraction of soul from all the concerns of this world; and sometimes a kind of vision or fixed ideas and imaginations of being alone in the mountains or some solitary wilderness, far from all mankind, sweetly conversing with Christ, and wrapped and swallowed up in God. The sense I had of divine things would often of a sudden kindle up, as it were, a sweet burning in my heart, an ardour of soul that I know not how to express.

To a mind open to beauty and already practiced in tracing the hidden reality behind the external forms, the charm of nature gave further intimations of God. Edwards had none of that sense of kinship with nature which permeates the writing of the later Romantic poets. He thought of nature symbolically. The loveliness of nature and its majesty suggested to his enraptured eye the lovely and majestic glory of God.

Nearly twenty years later he could recall the very occasion when, as he was alone in a solitary place, walking in his father's pasture, nature thus spoke to him in many voices. He was then about eighteen years old.

After this my sense of divine things gradually increased and became more and more lively and had more of that inward sweetness. The appearance of every thing was altered; there seemed to be, as it were, a calm, sweet cast or appearance of divine glory in almost every thing. God's excellency, his wisdom, his purity and love, seemed to appear in everything; in the sun, moon and stars; in the clouds and the blue sky; in the grass, flowers, trees; in the water and all nature; which used greatly to fix my mind. I often used to sit and view the moon for a long time; and in the day spent much time in viewing the clouds and sky, to behold the sweet glory of God in these things: in the meantime singing forth with a low voice my contemplations of the Creator and Redeemer. And scarce any thing among all the works of nature was so sweet to me as thunder and lightning; formerly nothing had been so terrible to me. Before I used to be uncommonly terrified with thunder and be struck with terror when I saw a thunder storm rising; but now, on the contrary, it rejoiced me. I felt God, if I may so speak, at the first appearance of a thunder storm; and used to take the opportunity, at such times, to fix myself in order to view the clouds and see the lightnings play and hear the majestic and awful voice of God's thunder, which oftentimes was exceedingly entertaining, leading me to sweet contemplations of my great and glorious God.

Doubtless this youthful experience was in his mind in his Thanksgiving sermon at Northampton in 1734: "the noise of thunder and the roaring of many waters are the most great and majestic sounds ever heard upon earth."

With such an intensely religious nature the only adequate career for Edwards was in the church.

After his graduation from Yale in 1720, therefore, he returned for a couple of years of graduate study in theology. Then having secured a license to preach, he accepted a call to a small Presbyterian church in New York City, where he remained, however, for only eight months. In retrospect this brief period seemed to him the most idyllic of his life. Three memories were sharpest: the friendship of the family with whom he boarded; his solitary walks along the unfrequented banks of "Hudson's River"; and his assiduous perusal of the newspapers in search of "news favorable to the interests of religion in the world." But the church was small, its future doubtful, and it was so heavily encumbered with indebtedness that even twenty years later it had not been able to afford to glaze all its windows, eight of them still being covered with boards. Edwards apparently came speedily to the conclusion that the church needed a leader more mature and worldly-wise than himself, and so resigned.

After spending the next summer at home studying, he accepted an invitation to return to Yale in the capacity of tutor. During the next three years his life was a combination of study, teaching, and administration. The burden of the last was particularly severe, as Yale was at that time without a rector. Edwards and the two other young tutors were to all intents and purposes in charge of the college.

Two more bridges still remained to be crossed before he could settle down firmly into his career.

The ministry was to be his vocation. But in what denomination should he work? Congregationalism was not only the established church in New England, but far and away the most dominant one. There was a scattering of Quakers and other sects, notably the Anglican. Episcopalianism had already drawn to itself the faculty of Yale—consisting of a president and a tutor—as well as three other ministers, to the consternation of the Connecticut churchmen. The movement gave evidence of possessing considerable vigor. Within less than twenty years there were over twelve hundred Episcopalians in the state. To a young man entering the ministry at this time the option was no longer closed. It was not a case of either a Calvinistic pulpit or no pulpit at all. So far as the external situation was concerned Edwards might have followed the example of Samuel Johnson and other fellow alumni of Yale, become an Episcopalian, gone to England to secure ordination, and returned to a small village church where he could have philosophized and written books to his heart's content. A fugitive entry in his Journal, written while he was a tutor, indicates his awareness of the option: "Friday, May 21 [1725], If ever I am inclined to turn to the opinion of any other Sect: *Resolved*, Beside the most deliberate consideration, earnest prayer etc., privately to desire all the help that can possibly be afforded me from some of the most judicious men in the country, together with the prayers of wise and holy men, however strongly persuaded I may seem to be that I am in the right."

Something more powerful than the help and prayers of holy men determined Edwards' choice of the Congregational ministry, and that was his philosophy. Episcopacy was tainted with Arminianism, as the theology of those who disagreed with Calvinism was popularly called. Samuel Johnson had already complained that this charge was false. None the less there it was. A relativistic theology, such as Arminianism, with its curtailment of the divine omnipotence in favor of human initiative and responsibility could hardly prove attractive to a mind like Edwards'. One to whom God was all in all could be satisfied with nothing less than an absolutistic theology such as Calvinism.

But the shift from a philosophy that thought of God in terms of absolute Mind and Being to a Calvinistic theology that thought of God in terms of absolute Will was an easy one. Such a transition by way of the feature of absoluteness common to both involved no emotional jarring or intellectual discomfort. In turning thus from philosophy to Calvinistic theology, however, Edwards did not surrender his philosophical interests; his philosophy, like his science, continued to exercise a dominant influence in his career.

Meanwhile Yale, after angling in vain for four different ministers, had finally persuaded Elisha Williams, Edwards' former tutor at Weathers-

CHOOSING A CAREER

field, to accept the rectorship of the college. Though he later became Edwards' bitter personal enemy, at this time, so far as is known, the relations between the two were entirely cordial. It was no more than a coincidence that Edwards resigned as tutor in 1726 at the very time Williams was inaugurated. The fact was that Edwards had now reached the age of twenty-three; he had had several fruitful years of graduate study; he had tried himself out as a minister; he wanted to get married; and—he had received a very flattering call to become the associate minister of the most important New England pulpit outside of Boston. The church in the rapidly growing town of Northampton, whose venerable pastor, the Reverend Solomon Stoddard, was Edwards' own grandfather, needed a young man as assistant with the expectation of eventually becoming the regular minister.

He had, apparently, received other calls. Indeed he had accepted one to Bolton, Connecticut, where the provision for the minister's support was characteristic of the period. The initial salary of sixty pounds was to be paid one-half in money and one-half in Indian corn and wheat at current money price. And each of the adult inhabitants was to work two days a year for three years in fencing and clearing for the new minister. For one reason or another he did not settle at Bolton but returned to Yale as tutor.

The call of the Northampton church, however,

Edwards accepted and he was ordained there on February 15, 1727. He was to face two more difficult decisions in regard to his career, the first of them twenty-three years later, but, so far as he now knew, he was settled for life.

Chapter Three

RELIGION COME ALIVE

The town of Northampton is of about eighty-two years standing, and has now about two hundred families; which mostly dwell more compactly together than any town of such a bigness in these parts of the country. . . . The people of the county in general, I suppose, are as sober and orderly and good sort of people as in any part of New England; and I believe they have been preserved the freest by far of any part of the country from error and variety of sects and opinions. Our being so far within the land, at a distance from seaports and in a corner of the country, has doubtless been one reason why we have not been so much corrupted with vice as most other parts.—
Narrative of Surprising Conversions.

At the time of his ordination in Northampton Edwards was twenty-three years of age. Six months later he rode down to New Haven to marry Sarah Pierrepont, the seventeen-year-old daughter of one of the founders and first trustees of Yale College. She was "comely and beautiful and of a pleasant agreeable countenance." Edwards may well have known her and even played with her as an undergraduate, but it was not until he became a tutor that he was impressed with her budding loveliness. The oddly one-sided description of her charm, which he had written when he was nineteen and she was thirteen, shows, for all its rapturous enchantment, a penetrating estimate of her disposition which their thirty years together did not change.

They say there is a young lady in ——— who is beloved of that Great Being who made and rules the world and that there are certain seasons in which this Great Being, in some way or other invisible, comes to her and fills her mind with exceeding sweet delight, and that she hardly cares for anything except to meditate on him—that she expects after a while to be received up where he is, to be raised up out of the world and caught up into heaven; being assured that he loves her too well to let her remain at a distance from him always. There she is to dwell with him and be ravished with his love and delight forever. Therefore, if you present all the world before her, with the richest of its treasures, she disregards it and cares not for it and is unmindful of any pain or affliction. She has a strange sweetness in her mind and singular purity in her affections; is most just and conscientious in all her conduct; and you could not persuade her to do anything wrong or sinful if you would give her all the world, lest she should offend this Great Being. She is of a wonderful sweetness, calmness and universal benevolence of mind, especially after this Great God has manifested himself to her mind. She will sometimes go about from place to place, singing sweetly; and seems to be always full of joy and pleasure; and no one knows for what. She loves to be alone, walking in the fields and groves, and seems to have some one invisible always conversing with her.

Underlying the union between Jonathan and Sarah Edwards was an auspicious community of interests as well as a capacity for sharing each other's loyalties, ideals, and faith. As they drew near to their God, they found themselves drawn nearer to each other.

Not long after their first child, Sarah, was born, Edwards' grandfather and colleague died in his eighty-seventh year. For two years these men had worked side by side, Edwards taking over rather more than half the preaching responsibility. Few events emerge from the obscurity of those early years of his ministry. A break-down in health necessitated his absence from the parish for several months. In 1731 he was honored by an invitation to preach at the "public lecture" in Boston. His vigorous sermon with its specific rejection of unorthodox views so delighted the leading Calvinistic ministers that they persuaded him to let them print it. Thereafter scarcely a year passed in which he did not publish a sermon, a tract, or a book.

Edwards remained all his life a good Calvinist, though his inquisitive and speculative mind ranged far beyond the boundaries of inherited theology and even within its circle his emphasis was such as to enrich and rejuvenate traditional thought. Of these new departures his first printed sermon was prophetic. To be sure, his main point was the familiar doctrine that God is glorified in man's dependence. He sounded a fresh note, however, in his remark that "the beauty of God will forever entertain the minds of the saints. . . . They are made excellent by a communication of God's excellency."

Fully as prophetic of days ahead was a revival of religion in Northampton. It was to provide him with one of the main objects of intellectual and emotional interest for a score of years. This was not his first experience of revivals. They had occurred from time to time in his father's church. But this was his first professional contact with one. To his colleague they were an old story. Mr. Stoddard could recall four previous "harvests," as he called them, during the sixty years of his ministry. His experience with them he had garnered up in a couple of brief volumes which he shared with his grandson.

These revivals of religion, however, had been tentative, sporadic, and local. Half a dozen years after Mr. Stoddard's death occurred another revival which, because of its far-reaching consequences, may be considered part of a movement that was spreading across the face of the whole Christian world. In Germany this larger movement goes by the name of Pietism; in England it is known as Evangelicalism; in America as the Great Awakening. It was the precursor of the Romantic movement which came to expression through such men as Rousseau in France; Goethe and Schleiermacher in Germany; Coleridge, Carlyle, and Wordsworth in England. These poets and philosophers carried the insights of pietism out beyond the confines of the church in which it was cradled, and applied them to the social and intellectual life of the secular world.

This general movement represented an emancipation from formalism, intellectualism, and moralism in religion. It refused to identify religion with forms and ceremonies. Religion was more than ritual. It declined to equate religion with theological propositions and correctness of belief. Religion was more than creed. It saw through the speciousness of the assertion that man's claim on life is satisfied when he becomes a good citizen or an honest and friendly neighbor. Religion was more than civics. Religion was seen to be the profoundly stirring response and reconstruction of an individual's whole nature in the face of the impressions of power, beauty, and goodness which God and the universe make upon him. Pietism found room for the emotions. It dignified the religious feelings. In New England the time was ripe for a revival of such religion. But the occasion waited upon a leader who should crystallize and dramatize the situation and force the issue. From Edwards' fiery spirit came the spark that set the ready tinder aflame.

The beginning of the Northampton revival of 1734-35 is shrouded in obscurity. Edwards' preaching must have been a major factor in its origin. But prior to 1733 he did not date his sermons, so that it is now impossible to trace the way in which, with cumulative effect, his preaching and leadership finally produced a revival of religion that in intensity far exceeded anything that had happened in Northampton in days gone by. Yet it is not difficult to reconstruct the affair in imagination once it was under way.

"How have you indulged yourself from day to day and from night to night in all manner of unclean imaginations!" Tall, pale-faced, gestureless, Edwards stood behind the preacher's desk on a Sunday morning in 1734 and announced as his text a phrase from the Epistle to the Romans: "That every mouth may be stopped." Some years later he came to count it his most effective sermon. When he sat down there were few in the congregation who could still think complacently of themselves. He named no names. But his words searched out individuals.

Look over your past life. . . . How little regard you had to the Scriptures, to the word preached, to Sabbaths and sacraments! . . . What wicked carriage have some of you been guilty of towards your parents! . . . What revenge and malice have you been guilty of toward your neighbors! Have not some of you allowed a passionate furious spirit and behaved yourselves in anger more like wild beasts than like Christians? . . . What covetousness has been in many of you! How much of a spirit of pride has appeared in you! . . . How have some of you vaunted yourselves in your apparel! Others in their riches! Others in their knowledge and abilities! How it has galled you to see others above you! How much has it gone against the grain for you to give others their due honor! And how have you shown your pride by setting up your wills and in opposing others and stirring up and promoting division and a party spirit in public affairs! . . . And what abominable lasciviousness have some of you been guilty of! . . . Your soul . . . has become a hold of foul spirits and a cage of every unclean and hateful bird. . . . And such company, where lascivious talk and unclean songs have been carried on has been your delight.

Small wonder that many believed him when he drew the conclusion that "men go to hell every day out of this country!" No one's back escaped the scourge of his words.

How have you neglected your children's souls! . . . What low thoughts you have had of God and what high thoughts of yourselves! Many of you by the bad examples you have set, by corrupting the minds of others, by your sinful conversation, by leading them into sin or strengthening them in sin and by the mischief you have done in human society other ways have been guilty of those things that have tended to other's damnation. . . . God has preserved you while you slept; but when you arose it was to return to the old trade of sinning. . . . If God should forever cast you off and destroy you, it would be agreeable to your treatment of himself, of Christ, of your neighbors and of yourself.

There was a directness, a passionate earnestness, and a searching indictment in this preaching such as Northampton was unaccustomed to. Ordinarily the villagers went to church on the Sabbath because there was nothing else to do. The church service offered a welcome relief from the routine drudgery of the week. The minister's lecture changed the current of their thoughts, giving both farmer and housewife something fresh to think about. The sermon served as newspaper, journal of opinion, historical novel, and debate all in one. During the service, to be sure, one might also chance to come face to face with those farther reaches of human experience that slip from the jaded sight of the workaday week. One might recover a sense of participation in the age-old experience of human living. One might come to realize the frailty and fragmentariness of this mortal life. After the service there were neighbors to meet and there was gossip to be exchanged.

So it had often been in the past. But the sermons Edwards was preaching all probed deeper. His strategy was not to make religion easy. He expected others to find the same fierce joy he himself experienced in doing something that it was just barely possible to do. Nor was he wholly mistaken in his strategy.

To be sure, when the benediction had been pronounced, the pew doors slatted open, and the congregation had begun to file out of the chilly meeting-house, there must have been some among the number whose faces were white with rage, for anger has always been a familiar device to which people have recourse when they find their self-esteem threatened. Others doubtless were nodding their heads in acknowledgment of the justice of the arraignment, only to discount it immediately by various excuses: what other behavior could you expect of me with a wife like mine, or with the kind of land I have to farm, or with my headache or my bad heart? Some of the members of the congregation probably hurried out intent on filling an engagement or finding something else to do, knowing that if they kept busy they could forget the grim picture of themselves which the preacher's words had conjured up before them for one bitter moment. Furtively a few must have sneaked off to the tavern, though this practice, as we shall see, became increasingly infrequent. There they could join with their cronies in snickering at the fantastic notions of the preacher. The wounds of his barbed words would heal in the companionship of friends who made fun of the ideals and standards he had for an instant made compelling.

But the majority seem to have responded to Edwards' appeals. We shall not be far wrong if we think of them leaving the church deeply troubled in spirit. It is, in fact, possible to construct a moving picture of their tortured thoughts that is psychologically true, even though lacking in historical documentation. Without a turmoil of heart on the part of many, the historical facts of the revival can be neither explained nor appreciated. How far Edwards' preaching was the cause and how far only the occasion of their perturbation cannot, of course, be determined. They must have marveled at the uncanny accuracy of his description of their behavior. Even so, perhaps he succeeded not because of the specific sins he enumerated so much as because he focused attention both on the unattained possibilities of good in his people's lives and on the growing strength of desires and tendencies they recognized as being potentially disastrous. He forced them frankly to face themselves, even though the sight they saw was well-nigh unbearable. "Consider what you are." So life reached a climax for one individual after another.

We may easily imagine how these men and women faced this crisis that threatened to destroy the already shattered integrity of their souls. Being temperamentally neither cravenly evasive nor resigned, they could not bring themselves to seek peace at the price their neighbors paid. They must endeavor to reconstruct their lives around some new principle of unity and purpose. But first of all they must talk their problem out. To whom should they turn for help? Why not to Mr. Edwards himself? He was known to be able to keep his mouth shut. But might it not be better to go to some friend who would be less likely than Mr. Edwards to pass judgment on them? No, they did not want sympathy and excuses. They wanted understanding. They craved objectivity of judgment. They needed counsel as to how to piece together the disjointed and damaged fragments of their lives. Above all, they wanted to come to terms with conscience in some more satisfactory way than just by throwing it out of the window. Perhaps it would be well to see Mr. Edwards.

After all, he stood in their eyes as the representative of their conscience and of the best in the community. He was a kind of symbol or at least a reminder of their God. Nothing less than the ultimate approval and support of that which they honored and loved, mediated through him, could heal their hurt. And even if he did nothing more than listen, he would help, for as they dumbly knew, confession is a kind of cure in itself, or at least the first step toward a cure, liberating one, as it does, from the awful isolation of a guilty conscience.

In agony of soul they knocked at the door of the parsonage, seeking counsel. The young minister soon found himself occupied with a kind of personal work that was a much greater drain on his vitality than study or the preparation and delivery of sermons. "The place of resort," according to his account of the affair, "was now altered; it was no longer the tavern but the minister's house that was thronged far more than ever the tavern had been wont to be." When the work was at its greatest height in March and April, he interviewed persons "at the rate at least of four in a day or near thirty in a week, take one with another, for five or six weeks together."

Fortunately—until his health again broke under the strain, forcing him to go away on a second recuperative trip—Edwards was able to put himself unreservedly at the disposal of these sick souls. The American preacher of the first half of the eighteenth century, unlike his twentieth-century counterpart, was not enmeshed in a network of miscellaneous duties. There was in Edwards' day practically no place in the ministry for the man whose major talent was a capacity to run organizations. The minister did not then have to carry on an elaborate program of religious education. Nor was he looked to as the leader in social reform.

So Edwards was able, without in any way jeopardizing the program of the church, to adjust himself to the new demand on his time. More than once in the early days of the revival the young pastor must have felt at a loss as to what counsel to give and how to handle the disturbed emotions of his visitors in the little study. Referring to cases of melancholia he frankly confessed, "One knows not how to deal with such persons." Fifteen years later he could see even more clearly his youthful lack of judgment and experience. "Instead of a youth there was want of a giant in judgment and discretion among a people in such an extraordinary state of things." At the time, though he exercised every caution, he was conscious of his inability to meet these spiritual problems with complete effectiveness. "I once did not imagine that the heart of man had been so unsearchable as it is." So he oscillated between moments of exaltation at his successes and of despair at his failures. Between appointments he must have conned the pages of Mr. Stoddard's *Guide to Christ or the Way of Directing Souls that are under Conversion.* When Timothy Ed-

RELIGION COME ALIVE

wards rode up from Windsor, as he frequently did, father and son no doubt engaged in discussions about the cure of souls that warmed the heart of each. But at best no one could have helped a man like Edwards very much, for his habit of shrewd and fresh observation, no longer confined to spiders and rainbows, prevented him from using stereotyped methods with his cases. He perceived too clearly the sharp differences and personal peculiarities of the individuals who came to him to treat them all alike.

The revival, once started, gained momentum with prodigious rapidity. The thing could not be hid. Reports of it reached even to England: Northampton in the Massachusetts Bay Colony is aflame with new zeal for God! Edwards was besieged with requests for information about what was going on in the little frontier town so far away from the centers of culture and commerce. His response was a small volume issued in the form of a letter, dated November 6, 1736, entitled, *Narrative of Surprising Conversions*. It was almost immediately reprinted in London by Isaac Watts. The adjective "surprising" indicates the tone of the book. No one was more amazed than Edwards. He did not try to explain or justify the revival. He simply told the story, with a skill in narration and exposition that sets him at once among the American masters of English prose.

Prefacing his narrative with a brief but charming description of the community, a part of which has already been quoted, he turned at once to the town's spiritual condition prior to the revival.

Just after my grandfather's death it seemed to be a time of extraordinary dulness in religion: licentiousness for some years greatly prevailed among the youth of the town; they were many of them very much addicted to night walking and frequenting the tavern and lewd practises, wherein some by their example exceedingly corrupted others. It was their manner very frequently to get together in conventions of both sexes, for mirth and jollity, which they called frolicks; and they would often spend the greater part of the night in them, without any regard to order in the families they belonged to: and indeed family government did very much fail in the town. It was become very customary with many of our young people to be indecent in their carriage at meeting, which doubtless would not have prevailed to such a degree, had it not been that my grandfather through his great age (though he retained his powers surprisingly to the last) was not so able to observe them.

Edwards did not say whether it was his sharper eyesight or something else that prompted the young people slowly but observably to grow more decent in their attendance at public worship under his own single ministry. He was young, handsome, brilliant, incisive, convinced, and convincing. He had a charming wife. The young couple must have been a welcome relief after the venerable Stoddard, who had seen most of the people in the town born and married but who had clearly lost touch with the rising generation. Furthermore,

Edwards could preach. To the surprise of their parents the "young of both sexes" agreed to his recommendation that they stay at home with their families in the evening, at least twice a week, after the public lecture and on the Sabbath. The young people also followed another of Edwards' suggestions that they assemble weekly "in various parts of the town and spend the evening in prayer and the other duties of social religion"; an example soon followed by their elders.

Meantime a controversy had arisen a few miles down the river at Springfield, where a brilliant but erratic young Harvard graduate, Robert Breck, was trying to get himself ordained. So violent did it become that the police had to be called in. Everyone in the neighborhood was "put into a ruffle" by it, according to Edwards, and was taking sides. He found it impossible to remain either aloof or silent, for an issue was raised which galvanized his mind into vigorous action. The gist of the question, as he saw it, was the reconciliation of the Calvinistic doctrine of the omnipotence of God with the personal responsibility of the individual. Some were insisting that since God has predestined certain persons to everlasting bliss, nothing further remains for them to do but to await it, and nothing can be done by the non-elect to secure the same blessing. Calvinism thus interpreted—or perhaps caricatured—issued in moral paralysis. Others, on the contrary, were insisting that a man's future is in his own hands; if he does not save himself he will not be saved. They were called

Arminians. Edwards opposed the doctrinaires on both sides. He found the passivism of the one thoroughly uncongenial to his active temperament and religious aspiration; he found the superficiality of the other equally distasteful. Men must be given an opportunity to act. Yet they must recognize that their activity cannot guarantee them success, for there is a mysterious fact of arbitrariness in the universe which precludes all calculable connection between effort and achievement not alone in the details of daily life, but also in the farther reaches of human hopes. Furthermore, the harder a man strives after moral excellence and the higher he sets his goal, the less satisfied is he likely to be with his efforts, until in the end he ceases to rely on himself and seeks spiritual reinforcement.

Out of Edwards' meditations on the apparent contradiction between these two great systems of thought, each of which offered a satisfactory interpretation of certain facts of experience and appealed in turn to different sides of his nature, came his solution. Both theories he concluded were equally true and untrue at the same time. He declined to accept an either-or. The dilemma of theory he resolved in the passionate paradox of life. His solution enabled him, he believed, to retain the significant features that lay in Calvinism, which the religious liberalism of the day seemed to threaten, and at the same time to utilize the undoubted values of the new emphasis. Such a point of view combined with the vigor of his mind and his emotional intensity made Edwards, quite without premeditation on his part, the prophet of a revival of religion.

He communicated his conclusions to his people in a series of sermons that they at once voted to publish. As he put it: God alone saves you, but he uses means to do so. Those means are your hearty desire for heaven, your firm resolution, your self-discipline and your obedience. You may not be saved if you engage in these good works, for you cannot bargain with the God of life; yet without them you will not be saved, either. "God must do all and yet we do all." He reminded them of the paradox lodged in the heart of the beatitude, the pure in heart see God, yet only those who see God can be pure in heart. So he urged them with all the persuasiveness at his command both to "press into the kingdom" and to let their faith alone count for righteousness.

For reasons now dimmed by the obscurity of the past this series of sermons he was preaching aroused the ire of his influential cousin, Israel Williams. "I was greatly reproached for defending the doctrine from the pulpit," said Edwards, but he kept right on doing so, to the intense displeasure of his cousin, whom his action seems to have alienated for life. This private controversy, together with the major conflict, thrust Edwards at once into a position of prominence and leadership which he proved himself quite competent to maintain.

"And then it was, in the latter part of December that the spirit of God began extraordinarily to set in and wonderfully to work amongst us." Several people were converted, among them a woman who had been "one of the greatest company keepers in the whole town." Edwards was excited. But he had already had sufficient experience with conversions to be somewhat skeptical of their genuineness and their influence. "Though the work was glorious, yet I was filled with a concern about the effect it might have upon others: I was ready to conclude (though too rashly) that some would be hardened by it in carelessness and looseness of life. But the event was the reverse to a wonderful degree." Religion had come alive.

Like a flash of lightning the revival struck the hearts first of the young people and then of their elders all over the town. "The noise amongst the dry bones waxed louder and louder. . . . The minds of the people were wonderfully taken off from the world; it was treated amongst us as a thing of very little consequence: they seemed to follow their worldly business more as a part of their duty than from any disposition they had to it. . . . Religion was with all sorts the great concern and the world was a thing only by the by." "In the spring and summer following, anno 1735," the narrative continues, "the town seemed to be full of the presence of God; it was never so full of love nor so full of joy and yet so full of distress as it was then. . . . Our public assemblies were then beautiful. The congregation was alive in God's service, every one earnestly intent on the public worship, every hearer eager to drink in the words of the minister as they came from his mouth; the assembly in general were from time to time in tears while the word was preached. . . . Our public praises were then greatly enlivened; God was then served in our psalmody in some measure, in the beauty of holiness." This must have particularly delighted Edwards, for he loved to sing. "Praise," he believed, "is the most joyful work in the world." That is why he looked forward with unfeigned pleasure to joining in "the glorious melody of heaven."

The revival had its ethical results as well. "Never, I believe," he concluded, "was so much done in confessing injuries and making up of differences as the last year. The tavern was soon empty. . . . People had done with their old quarrels, backbitings and intermeddling with other men's matters."

Even visitors to the town became infected with the new spirit and carried the contagion to neighboring communities. Under the guidance of Edwards' dramatic narrative we can see it spread from one river town to another and then to the neighboring hill towns until there was scarcely a village untouched in the Connecticut Valley from the Vermont border to Long Island Sound.

In Northampton the revival continued at high tension for about six months, during which time Edwards estimated that more than three hundred souls out of a total of six hundred and twenty communicants were "savingly brought home to

Christ." Edwards called attention to the fact that no two of these individuals had exactly the same experience. As once he had found pleasure in describing the habits of spiders, so now he gave himself with obvious enjoyment to the precise description and discriminating classification of the "frames of mind" of his people. He could not but note "vast differences in the manner and circumstances in which persons are wrought on." In consequence he was forced to disagree with "some good people" who were insisting that a conversion, to be genuine, must conform to a specific pattern. Edwards was never one to withhold or distrust the clear findings of his own thinking. "God," he said, "is further from confining himself to certain steps and a particular method in his work on souls than it may be some do imagine." Nevertheless he observed "a great analogy" in the steps of the experience of conversion. First of all—to mention only the two main features of his acute analysis—an individual is overcome suddenly or gradually with a sense of misery and guilt. Life looks "as black as midnight" to him. He feels that there is no help in him. He touches bottom. He recognizes that he has no claim on God; indeed he would like to kill Him. He gives up. Then, in the next place, comes the change to calm and composure and the recovery of power as the self-confessed sinner realizes that, though he deserves nothing, yet after all God does have something for him. Though he cannot help himself, if he will put his trust in God or Christ, he need no longer be fearful and distressed. Life will straighten itself out for him. Looking back upon his past, it will seem to him as though his former self with its old interests, standards, and practices had died. Now he is a new individual, facing a new world with a clear eye for its novelties. "The light and comfort which some of these converts enjoy gives a new relish to their common blessings and causes all things about them to appear as it were beautiful, sweet, and pleasant to them. All things abroad, the sun, moon and stars, the clouds and sky, the heavens and earth appear as it were with a cast of divine glory and sweetness upon them."

Eventually the excitement aroused by the revival subsided. Two of the townspeople committed suicide. Others had hallucinations. External events began to crowd on people's attention: "as particularly his Excellency the Governor's coming up and the Committee of the General Court on the treaty with the Indians; and afterwards the Springfield Controversy and since that our people in this town have been engaged in the building of a new meeting-house."

Yet there appears not to have occurred the widespread reaction and demoralization that might be expected to follow such an emotional excitement. Lasting changes in habit and attitude had apparently taken place. Writing a year and a half after the affair Edwards could say without qualification, "we still remain a reformed people, and God has evidently made us a new people"; and three years later, "in almost every household some have been made nobles, kings and priests unto God; some daughters of the Lord Almighty!"

With the ebbing of the tide of revivalism Edwards turned his attention to study and preaching. On March 13, 1737, he had just "laid down the doctrines" at the beginning of his sermon in the presence of a large congregation in the old meeting-house, when, without any warning, the front gallery gave way, tumbling with a noise like a clap of thunder on the heads of those that sat underneath. To the startled preacher it looked as though the falling gallery was "all broken to pieces before it got down." When the panic subsided and those who were buried under the heavy load of timbers extricated, it was found that beyond plenteous cuts and bruises no bones were broken and only one person internally injured. Edwards interpreted the event as "a most amazing instance of Providence" and set apart the following Wednesday to praise God for his mercy and to acknowledge in humility the divine warning and rebuke to the people.

This accident, together with the difficulty of providing seating accommodations for the three hundred new members who joined the church during the revival, brought to a head the building program that had first been broached three years previously. Among the several committees appointed in connection with the new building is one that deserves especial mention, the Seating Committee. Its primary task was to "estimate the pews and seats," that is, to determine the relative social value of the various locations in the auditorium; its next, to assign seats to people according to their respective social standing. The latter was determined first of all on the basis of wealth, then of age, and lastly of public usefulness. The chart which the committee prepared, and which is still extant, contains six hundred names. Whether or not Edwards had much to do with this phase of the enterprise, he could have found no fault with the principle employed. His own aristocratic theology, in fact, reflected the undemocratic spirit of the community.

During the first year in the new meeting-house Edwards preached a notable series of sermons on *Christian Love*, an exposition of the thirteenth chapter of First Corinthians. Though intended for publication, it did not find a printer for nearly a century. The next year he delivered an even more extensive and monumental series of thirty sermons on the subject of *A History of the Work of the Redemption*. In this novel outline of history, beginning with the fall of man and concluding with a prophetic glance toward the anticipated end of the world, Edwards took particular pains to emphasize every revival that occurred. Revivalism was near to his heart. No one could have been more exhilarated than himself when, a year later, in 1740, a revival of religion broke out on a scale that dwarfed the earlier affair at Northampton. That had been "done in a corner." The Great Awakening, as this fresh movement is picturesquely called, swept the length and breadth of the Colonies. It definitely and permanently changed the face of the American scene. Every community quivered with new life. Among its outstanding effects were the growth of a new humanitarian and missionary interest, the rise of the large denominations, and the impetus given to popular education. Now, perhaps for the first time, the inhabitants of the various Colonies became conscious that they belonged together as sharers of a common life.

Edwards threw himself ardently into the revival. Again and again he deserted his own pulpit to preach in neighboring towns. But the range of his direct influence was limited to the Connecticut River Valley. The outstanding figure of the day was the youthful Englishman, George Whitefield, under the impact of whose superb preaching the Great Awakening began. Like a shuttle of flame this unmatched orator, with his voice of perfect music, moved back and forth along the Atlantic seaboard from Savannah to Portsmouth, weaving together the fiery threads of local revivals and setting new fires ablaze. In the autumn of 1740 he stopped at Northampton to pay his respects to Edwards, who was already widely known in England on account of the earlier revival. Whitefield preached in Northampton five times and collected money for his orphanage in Georgia. During his visit Edwards took occasion to criticize his younger visitor for his uncritical reliances on "impulses" and his inclination to pass over-hasty judgments on unconverted people. Whitefield towered above

Edwards as a popular preacher. But when it came to intellectual acumen and theological ability, he shrank to dwarfish proportions alongside his host. Unlike much of the theological argument of the time, the discussion between the two men was quite friendly, and they parted with mutual respect and affection. "A sweeter couple I have not seen," said Whitefield of his host and hostess. Not long after this visit all the Edwards children—there were now seven of them—had a simultaneous attack of the measles. This episode made so deep an impression on Edwards that he noted it in the Record of the Family Bible. Yet it did not distract him long from the major interest of his mind.

Whitefield's superficiality has been adduced in explanation of the increase in irregularities attendant upon the new revival. But the seeds of disorder are latent in every such movement. Not even Edwards' local affair, though he kept it well in hand, was altogether free from hysteria. When the revival broadened out and developed leaders who felt little or no responsibility for the permanent spiritual well-being of those to whom they preached, the hysterical phenomena became more pronounced. On every hand critics arose. They multiplied attacks on the revival. They condemned both its theory and its practical consequences. In respect to the movement there was soon, as Edwards remarked, "no such thing as being neuters." Certainly he could not himself be neutral. Yet he could not indorse the movement without qualification. He was in the painful position of perceiving that both the critics and the champions of the revival had right on their sides. It was another case, he reflected, of Solomon's ships: "when they brought gold and silver and pearls they also brought apes and peacocks." The revival was a mixture of good and bad. The good was incontrovertible. But the recent manifestation of mischief and error was equally undeniable. Edwards decided to steer a middle course. "The great weakness of the bigger part of mankind," he observed, "in any affair that is new and uncommon, appears in not distinguishing, but either approving or condemning all in the lump. They that highly approve of the affair in general, cannot bear to have anything at all found fault with; and on the other hand those that fasten their eyes upon some things in the affair that are amiss and appear very disagreeable to them, at once reject the whole." He took upon himself the unpopular and ungracious task of criticizing the thing he held so dear. In his *Narrative of Surprising Conversions* he had assumed the impartial rôle of a reporter. The invitation to deliver the Baccalaureate sermon at the Yale Commencement, September, 1741, gave him his first opportunity, outside of Northampton, to speak as a critical apologist of revivalism. This discourse so favorably impressed the moderate champions of the movement that they had it published two months later under the compendious title, *The Distinguishing Marks of a Work of the Spirit of God, Applied to that Uncommon Operation*

RELIGION COME ALIVE 63

that has lately Appeared on the Minds of Many of the People of New-England, with a Particular Consideration of the Extraordinary Circumstances with which this Work is Attended.

As the adjective "surprising" betrayed the temper of Edwards' first book, so the adjective "distinguishing" characterized the attitude of his second. He declared that the revival was based on a sound theory but was subject to easy perversion by those who could not or would not recognize the difference between counterfeit and genuine religion. He deprecated the credulity with which the friends of the movement accepted everything that happened as a work of the Spirit of God. He also cautioned its opponents not to exaggerate the imprudences either in numbers or in significance. His tone throughout the book was one of authority. Had he not had wide opportunity for observing revivals in general? And was he not "intimately acquainted with soul concerns"? He concluded by giving the movement his ardent but discriminating approval.

His treatment of the subject forecast not only the general point of view, but also the method of two more pretentious books on the revival which he published in 1742 and 1746. The first of them was entitled *Some Thoughts Concerning the Present Revival of Religion in New England and the way in which it Ought to be Acknowledged and Promoted; humbly offered to the Public in a Treatise on that Subject.* John Wesley thought so highly of this book that he republished it in England in an abridged form three years later. Edwards was not content merely to acknowledge that some of the fruits of the revival were bitter and unwelcome. He was interested in finding out why it should produce such fruits. One explanation of its getting out of bounds he found in the youth and inexperience of many of its leaders. Nevertheless, he concluded that the good of the Great Awakening, as of the earlier affair at Northampton, far outweighed the evil. Business had improved. "More time has been saved from frolicking and tavern haunting, idleness, unprofitable visits, vain talk, fruitless pastimes and needless diversions, than has lately been spent in extraordinary religion; and probably five times as much has been saved in person's estates, at the tavern, and in their apparel, as has been spent by religious meetings." Furthermore, the poor Negroes and the Indians, "those wretched people and dregs of mankind," have been civilized. Vicious behavior on the part of young people which not even the laws and the vigilance of magistrates and civil officers had been able to restrain had dropped away. Edwards believed that "the new Jerusalem in this respect has begun to come down from heaven," and he was provincial and patriotic enough to think it quite appropriate that the new Jerusalem should land in America. He felt himself to be witnessing "the dawning of a general revival of the Christian church." In that he was not far wrong. It was, in short, "a glorious work of God." All the more necessary then that the revival be managed with intelligence and zeal.

Having been first the reporter of the revival, next its apologist and critic, he now assumed the rôle of organizer. He thought of himself as a kind of military staff-officer, whose business it was to engineer the movement. "We in New England are at this day engaged in a more important war" than that between England and Spain. With this end in view he proceeded to canvass the situation to discover more effective ways and means of forwarding the revival. He began to think now in terms of the whole English-speaking community in America. First of all he called upon all local and colonial government officials "cheerfully and vigorously to exert themselves to promote it," though, characteristically enough, the only specific measure he could suggest was the appointment of a day of public thanksgiving to God or a day of fasting and prayer, and the holding of public hearings on further procedure. He next turned his attention to the press. Newspapers were rare in New England and the publishing of books expensive and infrequent. But tracts and pamphlets could be struck off aplenty. "Great care should be taken," he urged, "that the press should be improved to no purpose contrary to the interest of this work"; though he did not go so far as to propose censorship or boycott.

Another suggestion Edwards made looked to the increase of the prestige and authority of the ministers. He was fearful, as well he might have been, lest the revival become a laymen's movement and thus slip into the hands of men even less competent than the ministers to give it a continuous expert leadership. He proposed to spike the guns of the critics of a professional ministry by the introduction of certain reforms in theological education. The emphasis he laid upon an educated ministry, a position inherited from the earliest traditions of the churches in New England, has ever since been a major tradition among Congregational and Presbyterian churches.

Colleges seem to have suffered then, as they do still, from what is perhaps an incurable academic affliction, an insufficiency of funds. Edwards saw no reason why heaven should be peopled mostly with the poor of this world. So he called upon rich men—"God has greatly distinguished some of the inhabitants of New England from others in the abundance that he has given them of the good things of this life"—to lay up for themselves treasures in heaven by endowing scholarships for ministerial students; or by establishing academies in poor towns and villages to increase the piety and raise the standards of secondary education; or by subsidizing the circulation of religious literature. Curiously enough, Edwards did not suggest gifts for the endowment of chairs of instruction or for the erection of buildings. The day of great material things in American education had not yet dawned. A college president was still a teacher rather than a money-raiser.

Edwards' program for the reorganization of the

revival betrays the scholar's touch. His was a pathetic gesture in the direction of reform. In common with his contemporaries he had little conception of the spasmodic character of revivalistic religion. He was not aware of its rhythmic nature, its ebb and flow. The reforms he proposed looked to a long continuation of the movement. Years would have been required to carry them out. What was needed was some immediate remedy, if indeed anything could have been done to control so widespread and spontaneous an outburst of religious emotion as the Great Awakening. Some of the leaders, in despair, drifted with the current. Others, disgusted by the abnormalities and irregularities which accompanied the movement, and fearful of its aftermath of disillusionment and moral laxity, gave themselves to the impossible task of trying to stem the tide or at least of keeping their own skirts clear. But Edwards was too sensitive to the human and divine values and aspects of the movement. Aristocrat in intellect though he was, conscious of his dignity as a member of the cloth, he was too realistic and too passionately interested in people both as psychological cases and as souls in misery, to wash his hands of it. "If this be not the work of God," he wrote to a friend, "I have all my religion to learn over again and know not what use to make of the Bible."

Chapter Four

RELIGION UNDER THE MICROSCOPE

William James characterized Jonathan Edwards' *Treatise Concerning the Religious Affections* as an "admirably rich and delicate description." There is a curious parallel in the development of these two Americans. Each turned from natural science to the science of psychology; from psychology in general to the psychology of religion in particular; and from the psychology of religion in general to abnormal religious psychology in particular. Here the parallelism ends. William James, in his *Varieties of Religious Experience*, took the attitude of a curious, not to say fascinated, observer. Edwards went farther. He was not only a curious observer, he was also an active participant. The experiences he studied he also shared much more intimately than did James. Furthermore, he wanted to bring his knowledge to bear on the very practical problem of saving souls who are "in the enemy's country." So he was not content just to satisfy his scientific curiosity, observing, classifying, and labeling the psychological phenomena of religion with disinterested impartiality. He proposed to separate the wheat from the chaff. He was seeking standards. Definitions are either descriptive or normative. They set forth an object as it is or as it ought to be and as it would be when at its best. Descriptive definition there is in Edwards' *Religious Affections* as plenteous, incisive, and fantastic as anything in James' *Varieties*. But sifting is there also. Some kinds of religion Edwards thought better than others. His book is a noble definition of religion at its best. It presents the most notable single discussion of religion America has produced.

This volume constitutes his fourth as well as most extensive treatment of the revival of religion. Originally delivered as a series of sermons in 1742 and 1743, it did not appear in published form until 1746, almost a decade after his first book on the subject. Its ragged and repetitious style betrays the excitement under which it was produced. Having enacted the rôle of reporter, critic, apologist and engineer of the movement, Edwards now became the theologian of it. What is religion? A good many things had happened during the course of the revival which had all been called religion. Edwards deprecated such an undiscriminating attitude. He was not skeptical of religion, but he suspected that much which people called religion had really little or nothing to do with it. In such a misunderstanding of the nature of religion he believed he had an explanation of the distressing and lamentable by-products of the revival. If he could show the leaders of the revival what they were really seeking, they might avoid some of its pitfalls and latent perils. A true interpretation of religion would serve as a criterion by which to test the genuineness of any supposed religious experience. It would be a pattern which ministers and laymen might set before themselves as the goal of their religious development.

Employing a stylistic device that he had already experimented with in his Yale sermon, he first examined a dozen different popular interpretations of religion. Though he mentioned no names, it is clear that in each type he had in mind specific contemporary leaders or schools of revivalistic theory. Successively he passed judgment on them all.

Here were certain ministers whose main objective was to stir up people's emotions. If only their hearers became excited enough so that they had an overpowering emotion of some kind that could be readily interpreted as love or fear of God, they were "saved." To anyone familiar with the technique of playing on the feelings such emotional attitudes were not difficult to arouse. Edwards himself had long been committed to a theory of religion in which large place was made for the emotions. Unlike many of his friends, he did not feel in the least inclined to rule religious experience out of court just because of its high emotional coloring. But is any titillation of the emotions religion? he queried. By no means. Nevertheless, it might be the accompaniment of a genuine experience and so should not be dismissed offhand.

Still other revivalists counted themselves successful if their hearers fainted, had fits, went into trances, cried out or otherwise lost control of their physiological mechanisms. To sober-minded people this sort of thing seemed patent evidence of lunacy or fraud. But not to Edwards. One might suppose that a person like Edwards, who had himself so well under control and who valued so highly the rational life, would have agreed with the critics of revivalism in condemning these bodily manifestations. The reason he did not repudiate them is perhaps not far to seek. The fact is that his own wife had on more than one occasion suffered bodily derangement as a result of her religious excitement. Edwards had already in an earlier book used her experience as a case-record, without, however, giving her name. This is her own account of her experiences: "Mr. Buell read two other hymns on the glories of heaven which moved me so exceedingly and drew me so strongly heavenward that it seemed as it were to draw my body upwards and I felt as if I must necessarily ascend thither. At length my strength failed me and I sunk down, when they took me up and laid me on the bed where I lay for a considerable time, faint with joy, while contemplating the glories of the heavenly world." On occasion her hands clenched and her body grew so chilly that her friends had to set her by the fire. At times she leaped from her chair, "with joy and exultation." She even went into trance-like states of ecstasy. "My heart and soul all flowed out in love to Christ, so that there seemed to be a constant flowing and reflowing of heavenly and divine love from Christ's heart to mine. And I appeared to myself to float or swim in these bright sweet beams of the love of Christ, like the motes swimming in the beams of the sun or the streams of his light which come in at the window. My soul remained in a kind of heavenly elysium."

In spite of these abnormal experiences Mrs. Edwards was a Christian gentlewoman. She ran her household with skill and brought up her eleven children with loving and intelligent care. She knew how to play the rôles of both Mary and Martha. Her home became for days at a time almost a boarding-house for visiting ministers. She even managed to fight down the jealous thoughts that beset her when she saw other preachers proving more successful than her husband, and in his own pulpit at that. She understood "how great a part of Christianity lies in the performance of our social and relative duties one to another." The pathological traits were facts, but her Christian disposition and behavior were also facts. Obviously the two sets of facts were not mutually exclusive. "If such things are enthusiasm," Edwards concluded, "and the fruits of a distempered brain, let my brain be evermore possessed of that happy distemper! If this be distraction, I pray God that the world of mankind may be all seized with this benign, meek, beneficent, beatifical, glorious distraction!"

Of the remaining common samples of contemporary misunderstanding of religion which Edwards presented, one more deserves to be cited, for it confirms his judgment tentatively expressed a decade before. The experience of conversion cannot be stereotyped. It differs in different people. Edwards had a very shrewd idea of the reason for the apparent uniformity.

It is to be feared, that some have gone too far towards directing the Spirit of the Lord and marking out his footsteps for him and limiting him to certain steps and methods. Experience plainly shows that God's Spirit is unsearchable and untraceable in some of the best of Christians in the method of his operations in their conversion. Nor does the Spirit of God proceed discernibly in the steps of a particular established scheme one half so often as is imagined. A scheme of what is necessary and according to a rule already received and established by common opinion, has a vast (though to many a very insensible) influence in forming persons' notions of the steps and method of their own experiences. I know very well what their way is; for I have had much opportunity to observe it. Very often, at first, their experiences appear like a confused chaos . . . but then those passages of their experiences are picked out, that have most of the appearance of such particular steps that are insisted on; and these are dwelt upon in the thoughts and these are told of from time to time in the relation they give: these parts grow brighter and brighter in their view; and others, being neglected, grow more and more obscure: and what they have experienced is insensibly strained to bring all into exact conformity to the scheme that is established.

Edwards was slow in getting to the heart of his subject. Indeed, the reader of the first two parts of the book is likely to catch himself wondering whether there is, after all, any such thing as genuine religion. It is not this, Edwards has insisted. It is not that. Such and such an experience may be a sign of genuine religion, but on the other hand it may not be a sign. On the whole, he succeeds quite effectively in sustaining the suspense until, in the final section of treatise, he is ready to proceed with a discussion of what religion is.

Religion is a particular kind of ethical and emotional response to a specific intellectual stimulation. Edwards did not allow himself to be victimized by a desire for simplicity. Then, as now, students of religion singled out one facet of the many-splendored thing called religion, treating that single feature as though it were the whole. According to the Protestant scholastics religion was orthodoxy; according to the liberals it was good conduct; according to the revivalists it was a kind of affection, or emotion as we should now say, for the word affection meant not affectionateness, but feeling. None of the common over-simplifications did Edwards countenance. To be sure, had one only the name of this book of his on the essence of religion, one might suspect him of having embraced the emotional theory which was rapidly gaining headway. The title—*A Treatise Concerning the Religious Affections*—is to some degree misleading; though quite unintentionally so. Religion, Edwards believed, could not be adequately understood unless it was comprehensively regarded. His own definition is succinct yet inclusive. It gives due place to the intellectual and ethical as well as to the emotional features of religion. "The essence of all true religion lies in holy love; and in this divine affection and an habitual disposition to it and that light which is the foundation of it and those things which are the fruits of it, consists the whole of religion." This definition alone would entitle Edwards to a prominent position among the philosophers of religion.

William James accounted Edwards among the empiricists because of his insistence that practice is the only sure evidence of genuine religion. The *Treatise*, according to James, is "an elaborate working out of this thesis." Edwards did, in fact, devote fully a quarter of his book to a discussion of the ethical aspect of true religion. The first question he wanted to ask of anyone who claimed to have had a religious experience was, has his conscience been touched? "That gracious affections have their exercise and fruit in Christian practice" he took to be axiomatic.

"The quintessence of religion is love." He found the theme of Christian love an inexhaustible subject for meditation. He dealt with it formally in an extended series of sermons as well as in a brief but notable *Treatise on Grace*, both of which were published posthumously. His discussion in the *Religious Affections*, however, is at once the most compact and analytical of the three. In none of them did he descend to sentimentality; in the last he strikingly transcended conventionality.

To be sure, he did single out the familiar trait of humility as a preëminent characteristic of love. Love is not puffed up. The reason for this is not far to seek. The sight of the beauty or goodness or greatness of the beloved one instills in every true lover a profound sense of his own unworthiness and lowliness. The God whom the Christian loves is perfect. As the Christian imaginatively sets before himself the divine perfection and measures the "whole of the distance [he] is at from that height" he cannot but feel humble. To people content with less than the best and willing to gauge their own standing or achievement by a relative rather than an absolute standard, the humility which Edwards proposed as a test would be meaningless.

Unfortunately, Edwards did not keep his discussion of humility on this high plane. A truly humble person, he said, behaves like a poor man.

A poor man is not disposed to quick and high resentment when he is among the rich: he is apt to yield to others, for he knows others are above him; he is not stiff and self-willed; he is patient with hard fare; he expects no other than to be despised, and takes it patiently; he does not take it heinously that he is overlooked and but little regarded; he is prepared to be in a low place; he readily honors his superiors; he takes reproofs quietly; he readily honors others as above him; he easily yields to be taught, and does not claim much to his understanding and judgment; he is not over nice or humorsome; and has his spirit subdued to hard things; he is not assuming nor apt to take much upon him, but it is natural for him to be subject to others. Humility is a kind of holy pusillanimity.

The historian can only surmise what were the experiences in his boyhood that account for this marked sentiment of inferiority and the lack of self-confidence which he commends, for such humility seems to have little or nothing to do with religious humility. This confusion between a pathological humility towards other persons and the wholesome, realistic humility of religion, has been one of the frequent errors of the religious mind.

Humility is only one of the traits of character which Edwards suggested as a test of the genuineness of religion. A Christian is likewise courageous. Fortitude consists in strength of mind exerted in two directions: "In ruling and suppressing the evil and unruly passions and affections of the mind; and in steadfastly and freely exerting and following good affections and dispositions without being hindered by sinful fear or the opposition of enemies." The last phrase of this sentence was prophetic of Edwards' attitude in stormy days that lay ahead. Still another test of genuine religion is indicated by his statement that "nothing can be invented that is a greater absurdity than a morose, hard, close, high-spirited, spiteful true Christian."

These criteria are not mentioned because they disclose any particular originality on Edwards' part. As a matter of fact, these and other similar tests which he includes represent the normal judgment of Christian people. They are significant chiefly because they show how steadily Edwards kept his head in the midst of the turbulent excitement of the Great Awakening. Its passions did not sweep him off the solid rock of Christian ethics.

He did, however, propose a further test which Christianity as a whole has infrequently employed. "Another thing wherein those affections that are truly gracious and holy differ from those that are false is beautiful symmetry and proportion." At so many points people fail to keep love's balance, and so fall short of genuine religion. "Some make high pretences and a great love to God and Christ . . . but they have not a spirit of love and benevolence toward men but are disposed to contention, envy, revenge and evil speaking; and will, it may be, suffer an old grudge to rest in their bosoms towards a neighbor, for seven years together, if not twice seven years." Others are not even-handed in their treatment of people. "They are knit to their own party, them that approve of them, love them and admire them; but are fierce against those that oppose and dislike them. . . . Some show a great affection to their neighbors and pretend to be ravished with the company of the children of God abroad and at the same time are uncomfortable and churlish towards their wives and other near relatives at home and are very negligent of relative duties. . . . Others pretend a great love to men's souls that are not compassionate and charitable towards their bodies. The making a great show of love, pity and distress for souls, costs them nothing; but in order to show mercy to men's bodies they must part with money out of their pockets." All such disproportionate conduct shows a want of balance that is essentially irreligious, for "there is symmetry and beauty in God's workmanship."

If the application to religion of the test of symmetry is out of the ordinary, the interpretation of love as disinterestedness is even more rare. Most people pray to God for profit. They seek some reward by serving him. Nevertheless, there are, in addition to those who worship God because he is good to them, others who worship him because he is good in himself. The saint, the connoisseur in religion, loves God for his own sake. His is an "unmercenary love of duty." With both these attitudes Edwards was familiar. "The grace of God may appear lovely in two ways: either as *bonum utile*, a profitable good to me, that which greatly serves my interest and so suits my self-love; or as *bonum formosum*, a beautiful good in itself." He had no doubts in his own mind as to which was the more truly religious attitude. He claimed that the man "whose affection for God is founded first on his profitableness to him begins at the wrong end." Like the lover of beauty, the lover of God is not calculating profits. No mercenary consideration enters in.

"The transcendently excellent and amiable nature of divine things" captivated Edwards' mind by a two-fold beauty. God was delightful and pleasant—both adjectives were frequently employed—because of his majesty and his holiness. Power and goodness have always been competing for the allegiance of human hearts, and to this day the battle is drawn and the palm unawarded. In fashioning their conception of God and in articulating their philosophies of life human beings select now one quality now the other as the more fundamental clue to the understanding of the world they live in. Power and goodness each tugged at Edwards' heart-strings. Again and again, both in this *Treatise* and in other books and sermons, he acknowledged the impression which the exhibition of divine power made upon him. He enjoyed the terrible majesty of God. The divine immutability was to him a source of exquisite pleasure. No mean religion, this! and one which people have turned to again and again when goodness has seemed to them an illusion, or an illegitimate hope. Better to worship a God who is real, though he be ruthless, than a God who is good only because he is imaginary. To Edwards the goodness of God was not an illusion. His own reflections and the authority of Scripture combined to convince him that God is holy. His power, his majesty, his greatness are enhanced and intensified by the fact that God employs his power in the interests of truth, righteousness, justice, kindness, and mercy. The Christian gospel itself, with its doctrines, its acts of Saviourhood, its words and works, was to him the most glorious sample of the powerful holiness of God. Here supremely is the moral beauty of God to be seen and enjoyed.

To many a modern the word "enjoy," as found in Edwards and in the Westminster Catechism's assertion that "man's chief end is to enjoy God forever," seems rather frivolous. But Edwards had the soul of an artist. He felt none of the conscientious objection of the mere moralist to a halt in activity for the sake of contemplating things lovely and of good report. If beauty is its own excuse for being, the appreciation of beauty needs not to be excused. Moralists may object to such a pause on the ground that it retards, if only momentarily, moral progress. To Edwards such contemplation is a significant feature of the religious life, the æsthetic or mystic moment it might be called, though he would himself have objected to either adjective. His writings are a reiterated protest against overlooking or minimizing this aspect of religion.

His declaration that the man who "closes with religion not for its own excellent name but only to serve a turn" has missed its secret is enough to mark him out as a genius among philosophers of religion. His mind sowed many an idea in the soil of the religious life of his generation, but none more fertile and reproductive than this use of the principle of disinterestedness as a criterion of true religion.

Edwards was well aware that this interpretation of religion in terms of disinterested love would not pass unchallenged. "Some say"—and it may be well to give at length his disarming and impregnable rebuttal, "that all love arises from self love and that it is impossible in the nature of things for any man to love God or any other being, but that love to himself must be the foundation of it. But I humbly suppose it is for want of consideration that they say so." His opponents should not be misled by that adverb "humbly" into thinking they were dealing with a tyro. "They argue, that whoever loves God and so desires his glory or the enjoyment of him, he desires these things as his own happiness. . . . And so, they say, it is from self-love or a desire of his own happiness that he desires God should be glorified. But then they ought to consider a little further and inquire how the man came to place his happiness in . . . contemplating and enjoying God's perfections. There is no doubt but that after God's glory and the beholding his perfections are become so agreeable to him that he places his highest happiness in these things, then he will desire them as he desires his own happiness. But how came these things to be so agreeable to him that he esteems it his highest happiness to glorify God, etc.?"

Edwards answered his question by asking another: "Is not this the fruit of love? A man must first love God or have his heart united to him, before he will esteem God's good his own and before he will desire the glorifying and enjoying of God as his happiness. It is not strong arguing that because, after a man has his heart united to God in love, as a fruit of this he desires his glory and enjoyment as his own happiness, that therefore a desire of this happiness of his own must needs be the cause and foundation of his love; unless it be a strong arguing that because a father begat a son therefore his son certainly begat him." That is to say the principle of self-interest is of only secondary importance in religion as it is also in æsthetics. Once an individual has come to love beauty and knows how beauty ministers to his need of permanence, poise, stimulation, and escape, he will in his own interest deliberately put himself in beauty's way. But this does not account for the initial impression beauty makes upon the human mind. At the first sight of beauty one has no experience to go by. One does not know that beauty feeds the soul. One only knows that it is something altogether lovely and one yields to it.

In view of the fact that Edwards is commonly though inadequately known as the preacher of "hell-fire" sermons whose appeal is almost wholly directed to the self-interest of his hearers, his insistence on the unmercenary love of God deserves especial emphasis. He did, to be sure, preach sermons of a calculating type. Only a year or so before he composed the first draught of his *Religious Affections* he had achieved an undying fame, or rather notoriety, by telling the people at Enfield, Connecticut, "The God that holds you over the pit of hell, much as one holds a spider or some loathsome insect, abhors you and is dreadfully provoked. O sinner! consider the fearful danger you are in."

Edwards preached countless sermons. Over a thousand of them were transmitted to his literary executor at his death. Had he not, among so many, preached from time to time on the fear of God and appealed to his people's self-interest, he might have laid himself open to the suspicion of abnormality. The "hell-fire" discourses do not, however, bulk large when his sermons as a whole are taken into account. They are far from typical. The principle of the uncalculating love of God found frequent and ample expression. As a matter of fact Edwards played upon the whole gamut of human sensitivity, varying his touch to strike different moods and tempers. That he appealed to the hope of reward and the fear of punishment primarily during the periods of intense revivalistic excitement, would seem to indicate that he was carried along by the spirit of the movement into a position that was far from representative of his best thought.

His analysis of the principle of religious disinterestedness led him to distinguish it in still another way. Disinterestedness is the opposite not only of a mercenary spirit, but also of sentimentality. He had observed people who were not so much in love with God as in love with being in love. They never forgot themselves, whereas "a true saint when in the enjoyment of true discoveries of the sweet glory of God and Christ has his mind too much captivated and engaged by what he views without himself to stand at that time to view himself and his own attainments: it would be a diversion and a loss, which he could not bear, to take his eye off from the ravishing object of his contemplation, to survey his own experience and to spend time in thinking with himself, what a high attainment this is and what a good story I now have to tell others. . . . What a good experience is this! What a great discovery is this! What wonderful things I have met with! And so they put their experiences in the place of Christ and his beauty and fullness. . . . They take more comfort in their discoveries than in Christ discovered."

Edwards' study of the principle of disinterested love led him to perceive an even more significant feature, its spontaneity. To love is not a matter of choice or of deliberate effort. Love is an involuntary, almost automatic, response to what is lovely and lovable. Love is our spontaneous tribute to beauty. "A holy person is led by the Spirit as he is instructed and led by his holy taste and disposition of heart. . . . He knows as it were spontaneously and of himself without a particular deduction by any other arguments than the beauty that is seen and goodness that is tasted. . . . He that truly sees the divine transcendent supreme glory of these things which are divine, does as it were know their divinity intuitively," without being at any trouble of a train of reasoning. Edwards' favorite analogy for this experience was the tasting of honey. No argument is needed nor can any prove that honey is tasty.

He was well aware that such reliance on intuitive knowledge of the value of spiritual objects opened the door to grave misunderstanding and abuse; especially so during a time of religious excitement. Many of his contemporaries, as well as predecessors, were guilty of misinterpreting this mystic way of gaining knowledge. He lumped together Montanists, the followers of Mrs. Hutchinson, "the many wild enthusiasts that were in England in the days of Oliver Cromwell and the many kinds of enthusiasts of the present day." He also included the Quakers, failing, in company with most of his contemporaries, to understand and do justice to their testimony to the Inner Light. Theirs was "bastard religion." Edwards, it is clear, had taken to heart Locke's famous chapter on Enthusiasm he had read so eagerly in college. To many of his present-day readers Edwards himself will seem to belong among these mystics and to be liable to the same charge of credulity as they. For his own part, however, he believed that he had found a method which avoided the fatal subjectivism of the mystic way. He proposed to submit every alleged intuition to two tests.

The first of these tests was ethical. It is frequently employed among positive mystics. It looks to the moral effects produced by the intuition. Unless the insight whose very spontaneity seems to guarantee its authenticity is ethically incandescent its source is not in God. The mind's love and knowledge of God, the *amor intellectualis dei* of the mediæval mystic, is not solely appreciation. It has moral dynamic. Since God is not only Absolute Idea or Truth but also Ultimate Power, the self-communication of himself which from the human side is apprehended as a holy taste is not only illuminating, but also energizing. Edwards frequently called it "a spring of action." Unless such an intuition issues in holy living, it is incorrect to attribute its origin to the indwelling of the Holy Spirit. This proposition takes us back to the central thesis of the *Treatise*. His emphasis on Christian conduct is hereby given its theological interpretation and justification.

Important as such a test is from the point of view of ethics, it has no significance from the point of view of logic. So he proposed a second criterion with a view to meeting the claims of logic. It was this: knowledge gained by the mystic way of intuition must not contradict the Bible. "Spiritual understanding does not consist of any new doctrinal knowledge or in having suggested to the mind any new proposition not before read or heard of. . . . This making of a new meaning to the Scripture is the same as making a new Scripture." In his private notes he put it even more sharply and paradoxically: "The discovery of God's spiritual glory is not by an immediate intuition but the word of God is the medium by which it is discovered." At first glance this test seems no more logical than its predecessor. Yet it is not so narrow or inappropriate as might appear, for to Edwards as to most of his generation Scripture contained the main body of known truth. To insist, as he did, that an intuition should not contradict Scripture was to insist that it harmonize with the body of common knowledge which constitutes the world of reason. What he conceived such an intuition to be was not the glimpse of some new item of knowledge, but rather a new appreciation and understanding and enjoyment of facts or doctrines already quite familiar but deficient in motive power because their significance had previously not been apprehended.

Later logicians may question the validity of this particular criterion, yet they will applaud the rationalistic and empirical temper in Edwards that prompted him to subject the reports of the mystic to the most rigid testing of which he was at the time capable. Nor will the logician fail to accord to the uncorroborated intuitions of so great a genius in the field of religion the same respect he would show to the similar intuitions of persons of "intellectual good-taste" in the field of philosophy or science. Indeed, it may well be that he will think Edwards over-hesitant and timid in his reliance upon the mystic way of knowledge.

Edwards' interrogation of religious mysticism had other motives than an interest in logic. On the strength of their intuitions enthusiasts all about him in New England were breaking away from the established order of religion and setting up separatist meetings of their own. As a duly authorized minister of the established church Edwards was loath to see it forced to surrender any of its power and prestige to such irresponsible groups. Many different arguments were brought by the official leaders of the churches against these separatists. It was due to his peculiar concern for ethics and logic that he chose to attack them as he did. Like them he was a mystic, but his was a critical mysticism, as critical, in fact, as the intellectual assumptions of his time and place permitted.

For him seriously to set up such a high logical and ethical standard for the religious life is cause for wonder, if not for despair. That he could do so was due in part to his theology. He believed, on the basis of his own experience and the report of others, that God could be trusted to communicate sufficient of his light and power to make such religion possible. On the other hand, he did not expect God to perform the incredible task of communicating his holiness to everybody. This revelation would come only to an elect minority. An aristocratic theology provided a fitting basis for his aristocratic and lofty religion.

Chapter Five

PLAY AND WORK

"I am fit for no other business but study," Edwards once wrote to an acquaintance. His friends thought of him as the scholar in the pulpit. He was reputed to spend thirteen hours a day in his study. Of course there were interruptions, yet his work gave him so much pleasure that interruptions were a cause of regret rather than of delight. Many of the ordinary avenues of recreation were closed to him. Frail in body and subject to frequent periods of illness, he could not indulge in sports even if the conventions of the day had sanctioned ministerial athletics. How much diversion he found within the family circle is far from clear. History has an unfortunate way of neglecting to record the little things which might serve as clues to the human side of its heroes. What kind of relaxation did he indulge in after supper in the midst of his constantly growing family? Did he consider the reading of the occasional newspaper or periodical that found its way into the house work or play? In an ordination sermon he urged a candidate to follow Christ's example in taking "gracious notice from time to time of the little children." Was Edwards as attentive to boys and girls outside the pulpit as he was in his preaching? Did he play much with his own children? On whose initiative was the purchase of "1 child's plaything, 4/6," his or his wife's? How much pleasure did he find in her companionship? A fugitive scrap of paper, tucked in one of the many packages of manuscripts, letters and other documents which constitute his literary remains, consists of a bill for "a gold locket and chane costing £11." In celebration of what event did he present this gift to her?

Almost daily his wife's knock at the door meant a brief and welcome interruption of his formal study. According to the account given by Samuel Hopkins, who spent some time in the Edwardses' home as a theological apprentice, "he was wont frequently to admit her into his study and converse freely with her on matters of religion; and he used commonly to pray with her in his study at least once a day, unless something extraordinary prevented."

Sarah Pierrepont Edwards was lovely to look at. She was even lovelier to live with. There was nothing "stiff and starch" about her. Whatever deficiencies her husband may have had in humor and gayety, she amply compensated for. Not even her frequent periods of physical suffering quenched her cheerfulness. Proud of her husband—sinfully so, she felt at times—she devoted herself to him. Without her constant care and fending it would have been impossible for him to live as long and accomplish as much as he did. Edwards was far from robust. His life was checkered with illnesses. She was "a tender nurse to him." She watched over his diet.

Occasionally he concerned himself with domestic problems. In the matter of the purchase of ninety pounds' worth of sheep he conducted quite a correspondence with Joseph Bellamy, displaying therein the instincts of a good trader. But for the most part Mrs. Edwards assumed the management of the household affairs, within doors and without, proving herself to be "a judicious and faithful mistress of a family, habitually industrious and a sound economist." How much help she had in her domestic activities is uncertain. Part of the time one of the innumerable cousins helped out. Edwards once records the death of a faithful servant, and among his "quick stock" at his own death was said to be a negro slave. At any rate, his wife so managed that he was as free as he cared to be to devote himself to the work he was most fitted to do.

Mrs. Edwards brought up eleven children. In this she showed herself extremely skillful. Visitors at the Edwardses' home, noting the number of children—Sarah, the oldest, was, to be sure, twenty-two when Pierrepont, the youngest, was born—marveled at her poise and soft-speaking. She never had to shout at them, according to Hopkins, though it seems incredible. From the beginning she tried to train them in ways of independent judgment and reasonableness, always explaining to them why she asked them to do thus and so. She taught them to pray. "When she met with any special difficulty in this matter," to quote again from the student, who never forgot his happy days in her household, "she was wont to apply to Mr. Edwards for advice and assistance." Fortunately they saw eye to eye in these matters. They did not, as Edwards put it, "weaken one another's hands in this work, one parent disapproving what the other doth; one smiling upon a child while the other frowns; one protecting, while the other corrects. When things in a family are thus," he added, "children are likely to be undone."

Edwards took these activities of his wife for granted. His mother had been the same sort of competent and thrifty person, noted for the way she had relieved his impractical father of the routine duties of a home. He believed in family government and thought of himself as the head of the family, though a visitor might have observed that the stability of the government depended to an equal degree on the able primeminister, his wife. For all his notions of male supremacy, he was far from taking a condescending or authoritarian attitude toward her. Was she not his spiritual equal, one with whom he enjoyed a delightful comradeship? Together they collaborated both in the work of the parish and in their philanthropies. When he preached against husbands who "treated their wives like servants by laying them under unjust and unreasonable restraints in the use and disposal of their common property," his parishioners knew he did not behave that way himself. If he spoke of occasions when husband and wife, after "a misunderstanding is begun are guilty of exasperating the other's spirits by unkind language until each of them blows up as a spark into a flame," his hearers must have wondered where he learned that such things happen. When he asked them, "Do you endeavor to accommodate yourself to each other's tempers? Do you study to suit each other?" they had the impression that he had already practiced what he preached.

The reverse side of a page of one of his sermon manuscripts hints at one of his forms of recreation. It is the record of the purchase of "1 dozen of long pipes." Did he buy them for the use of visiting ministers and laymen or for himself? How frequently did he resort to the consolation of tobacco? To one of his friends we owe our knowledge of his usual recreations. In winter he spent about half an hour daily chopping wood. In summer he went for walks and rode horseback, sometimes with Mrs. Edwards, oftener alone. "He would commonly, unless prevented by company, ride two or three miles after dinner to some lonely grove, where he would dismount and walk a while." Yet he probably failed to get from this exercise the complete shift of attention and interest so vital to good health, for he took his thoughts with him, as well as pen and ink to record them. Like many another author, he made a practice of jotting down his ideas as they came to him, not because he was intellectually so penurious that he must treasure each rare flower of thought, but because his mind was so fertile that he could not trust it to retain everything. To assist his memory when he could not use pen and ink on these rides he invented a curious device. Whenever he had an idea he pinned a small piece of blank paper to his coat to remember it by. Sometimes he returned home from his ride looking as though he had been out in a fall of soft snow. Once home in his study, he found these snippets of paper still charged with associative power. As he unpinned himself he wrote the ideas down.

Often these horseback rides carried him far afield. Edwards was in constant demand as a preacher of ordination sermons. He had to participate in council meetings of churches. He made it his regular practice to go to the Yale Commencement in the fall and the ministers' convention at Boston in the spring immediately after the general election. Twice a year he attended the meeting of the Hampshire County Ministers Association, which met occasionally rather far from Northampton, for Hampshire County at that time included all the territory now known as Hampshire, Hampden, and Franklin Counties. The minutes of these meetings, covering the period from 1731 to 1745, during which Edwards at times acted as scribe, are the precious possession of the Forbes library in Northampton. The mainstay of these gatherings, which ordinarily lasted the better part of three days, was the discussion of papers read by the members in turn, usually on theological or ecclesiastical topics, which were assigned six months ahead. Among the themes to which Edwards and his colleagues addressed themselves were the perennial problems of ministers' meetings everywhere: methods of increasing piety in the churches, missionary collections, requirements for ordination, best methods of dealing with the dying, the difference between justification and sanctification. They discussed the evidences of Christian salvation, the validity of Roman Catholic baptism, the nature of the sin against the Holy Ghost, the ways in which Satan transforms himself into an angel of light, "what is meant by enthusiasm when the word is used in an ill sense," the true notion of a lie. They took steps to prevent the increase of missionaries from the Church of England. It can hardly be doubted that the pastor of the First Church in Northampton participated earnestly and vigorously in these discussions, even though it be recognized that there were ranges of his thought far removed from themes like these.

Topics of another sort lent variety to the programs of the Association. It acted as a kind of unofficial court of appeal in cases of local ecclesiastical discipline. The New England churches at this time took seriously their disciplinary function. This was a phase of the ministry which Edwards on more than one occasion acknowledged to be excessively difficult if not irksome. No record exists of his having sought the advice of the Association in problems of discipline, though he might have

PLAY AND WORK

done so in the case of a young Northampton man who expressed his contempt for the church by reading midwives' books or of another who declared that he wouldn't worship a wig. He seems to have consulted his uncle, Colonel John Stoddard, on such occasions. His colleagues, however, not infrequently brought their disciplinary problems to the group: "whether or no in case a young woman who has been guilty of stealing a silver snuffbox of her neighbor's and she afterwards has been seen to have the box, pretending to have found it in the street . . . ought not now for the glory of God and the peace of her conscience to make a public confession of these her crimes? Voted in the affirmative."

Still another objective for a horseback ride was East Windsor. Frequently he jogged down the river to preach for his father. Often he took one of his children with him. Once Mary was invited to accompany him on an even longer trip. Together they rode on horseback all the way to Portsmouth, New Hampshire. There Edwards had one of the few amusing experiences that the records of his life contain. They were late in arriving at the town and the service of ordination at which he was to preach had already begun. They entered the church as prayer was being delivered and Edwards tiptoed so quietly onto the platform that the man who was praying did not hear him but went right on, thanking the Lord for the gifts of piety, preaching, and intelligence possessed by the absent brother who was to have preached to them. He even added a word about Mary, who, though "a very worthy and amiable young lady, was still, they had reason to believe, without the grace of God and in an unconverted state." Edwards, meantime, was sitting uncomfortably on the platform, listening to this flattering eulogy of himself. When the prayer was over the leader discovered his presence. Showing no loss of composure, he turned to him, his hand out, and addressed him: "Brother Edwards, we are all of us much rejoiced to see you here today, and nobody probably as much so as myself. But I wish that you might have got in a little sooner or come a little later or else that I might have heard you when you came in and known that you were here. I didn't intend to flatter you to your face. But there's one thing I'll tell you: They say that your wife is going to heaven by a shorter road than yourself." At which Edwards bowed gravely, proceeded to the pulpit, and announced his text.

In his study the first claim upon his time was the writing of his weekly sermons and lectures. Edwards was a man of intellectual integrity. He did not skimp his preparation. He was a meaty preacher, constantly feeding the minds of his people and giving them much to think about as well as stirring their consciences. Though his published discourses are good examples of the lavish way in which he packed his preaching with ideas, they do not adequately indicate the wide range of his homiletical interest. Early in his ministerial career he determined not to devote too much time to the composition of his sermons. Did he perhaps recognize in himself such a disposition to refine and improve and elaborate a subject that, unless curbed, would finally cause him to spend the whole of a week in the composition of his regular sermons? The larger portion of his time he devoted to general study, with no thought of the specific public occasions to which he might put his results. Out of this rich treasure of painstaking and variegated investigation eventually came books and articles in great profusion.

Edwards was an omnivorous reader. In a drawer in his study he kept a notebook in which he wrote down titles, authors, and comments gleaned from reviews, from advertisements in periodicals and the backs of other books, and from the conversation and letters of his friends. This little book is still in existence, and constitutes one of the prize pieces of Edwardeana in the library of Yale University. It is a homemade notebook about eight by ten inches in size. Many of the seven hundred entries have been scratched out with vertical or horizontal lines; some have X's alongside them. Recently the complete manuscript has been deciphered and the symbols plausibly interpreted— a difficult task on two accounts, for though Edwards could write legibly enough when necessary, the writing intended solely for his private eye is anything but clear. And nowhere does he indicate what he means by his marks and scratches.

Whenever he heard about a book that interested him enough to want to see it or buy it, he jotted down its title in the notebook, often adding a brief characterization of its contents. If at some later time he had an opportunity to read it he scratched it off his list. Taken in connection with the references to various authors in Edwards' published works, the notebook presents a kind of literary autobiography of its author. He listed over a score of books on science, showing that his early interest never waned, but prompted him to keep up with advances in that field. Among them are several of the works of Sir Isaac Newton, including the *Principia*, fifteen or sixteen books on geography, and a treatise on experiments in physics. Perhaps it was with the help of the last named that he measured the near-by Mt. Tom and found it to be sixty-three rods high. In the year 1752 he made a note "to enquire after some Philosophical Treatise of the Nature of Electricity, the best that is extent." Benjamin Franklin was engaged in his experiments at this time and the colleges were introducing lectures on "the newly discovered element, the electrical fluid." Early in the notebook appears a book on etiquette, *The Gentlemen's Library and Ladies' Library*, "published by Sir Richard Steele, containing rules of conduct for all parts of life," and another on sex. Later there is a *Dictionarium Domesticum being a complete Household Dictionary showing the whole art of cookery-art of making all sorts of English wines—the art of managing bees*. Still later, perhaps as his children grew older, he listed a collection of prayers for children and volumes with such titles as *The mathematical sciences abridged and made easy to the meanest capacity Designed chiefly for the use of Young Persons of Quality.*

In the field of literature he put down tools like Isaac Watts' *Art of Reading and Writing English,* and an *Essay upon Study wherein Directions are given for the due Conduct thereof & the Collection of a Library for the Purpose consisting of the Choicest books in all the several parts of Learning.* He noted, but apparently did not see, a new book on shorthand. Poetry and essays attracted him. He seems to have read Addison's *Essays,* Pope's *Homer,* Milton's *Paradise Lost,* as well as a collection of *Hymns and Sacred Poems* by John Wesley and at least one anthology of poetry. Three novels are mentioned, two of which, *Clarissa* and *Pamela,* he read. From another source we know that he also read *Sir Charles Grandison.* He quoted a review of the first, highly commending it as "embodying much to promote virtue and piety."

Three-quarters of the titles in the notebook deal, as might be expected, with religion. They cover a wide range of biblical, historical, and theological material. Edwards' hunger for books was never appeased. On one occasion the town voted an addition to his salary for the purchase of books. It was soon expended. Distances were too great for him to make use of the libraries of Harvard and Yale, such as they were. More immediately accessible was the coöperative library formed by the fourteen ministers who composed the County Association.

Most of the time he was in his study he devoted to scholarly investigations. To be sure, he was primarily a practical minister rather than a scholar. With few exceptions the subjects he studied were among the immediately perplexing problems of his day. Yet he handled these themes rather like a scholar than a minister. He offered no easy homiletical solutions. As a result his books were not just tracts for the time, useful today and forgotten tomorrow. He sought to get at the principles which underlay each specific problem and then to bring to bear upon its solution the learning and perspective of an historically and philosophically minded scholar.

There were exceptions to this practice. Such, for instance, was a book widely known in his day and frequently reprinted but now among the least read of his works. Its title is: *An Humble Attempt to Promote Explicit Agreement and Visible Union of God's People in Extraordinary Prayer, for the Revival of Religion and the Advancement of Christ's Kingdom on Earth, pursuant to Scripture Promises and Prophecies Concerning the Last Time.* A group of his friends in Scotland had conceived the idea of organizing prayer "for the advancement of Christ's kingdom." Edwards seized upon the proposal with eagerness. He commended it to his fellow ministers. He wrote about it. He preached a series of sermons designed to describe it, to justify it, and to answer objections to it.

Though he believed the day was not far distant when God would begin to usher in his kingdom, he had great need to buoy up his courage. The revival had petered out. "The present state of things in New England," he wrote a Scotch friend in 1744, "is indeed on many accounts very melancholy." In such events, however, as the suppression of the rebellion in Scotland, the complete destruction of the French Armada and the partial destruction of the French East India trade, he found patent signs of God's presence, which seemed to justify the belief that "the tide was turning and glorious things approaching by the revolution of the wheel of God's Providence."

Even genius does not strike out a fresh trail for itself in many directions. In this book, as in many another treatise, Edwards merely reproduced traditional ideas and attitudes of the Christian movement. No more than any of his contemporaries did he see fit to question the conventional Protestant attitude toward the Roman Catholic Church. He believed as a matter of course that "papists are found to injure, persecute and destroy the Protestant Church as much as in them lies." The same is true of his interpretation of the book of Revelation. He shared uncritically the traditional Christian view. The same might also be said of a number of the doctrines of his theology, which a full-length portrait of Edwards would necessarily have to deal with. Yet perhaps it is not so much what a man echoes from the past, but the new voice in which he speaks to the present, that is the proper subject-matter of history. The continuity of thought and practice may almost be taken for granted, so great is the inertia of the social mind. The same points of view reappear in generation after generation, with but slight modification. This is not to say that these ideas are not vitally held at the time. They are. They form a significant portion of the living body of conviction. But it is the new departures, the novel emphases, the fresh notions which a thinker puts into circulation, that entitle him to be singled out by the historian for consideration.

An altogether different kind of writing was his biography of David Brainerd. With momentary reluctance he had yielded to friendly requests that he edit the memoirs of this extraordinary missionary, for it meant setting aside temporarily another work that he was very eager to complete. His interest in Brainerd was both personal and professional. He had first become acquainted with him at New Haven when Brainerd had consulted him regarding steps to be taken to reinstate himself in Yale College, from which he had been expelled for attending a meeting of a separatist sect and for making uncomplimentary remarks about a member of the faculty. Brainerd came to conceive a profound admiration for the author of the *Religious Affections* and an even deeper regard for the latter's daughter, Jerusha, fifteen years his junior. During the whole period of his remarkable and exciting missionary labors among the

Indians in western Massachusetts and "near the forks of the Delaware" young Brainerd was constantly harassed by an infection of the lungs which he did nothing to alleviate. Finally in an advanced state of tuberculosis he was forced to give up the work he had so promisingly begun and to return to New England. There he made the Edwardses' already crowded home his headquarters. Jerusha took care of him. A few days before his death as he lay in bed he looked up "very pleasantly" at the girl who had nursed him so devotedly for nineteen weeks: "If I thought I should not see you and be happy with you in another world I could not bear to part with you. But we shall spend a happy eternity together." With this promise as her only reward and consolation, eighteen-year-old Jerusha herself soon fell fatally ill, the only one of Edwards' children who did not survive him. Her body was buried beside her lover in the "burying place" on Bridge Street.

Edwards reciprocated his young colleague's admiration and respect and his estimate of him throws light on his own scale of values. The *Memoirs* call attention to Brainerd's insight into human nature, his social disposition and agreeable conversation, his power of communicating his thoughts, and his "talent for accommodating himself to the capacities, temper, and circumstances of those whom he would counsel or teach." Edwards thought Brainerd's manner of praying in the family almost inimitable, for he "expressed himself with such exact propriety and pertinency, in such significant, weighty, pungent expressions, with such an appearance of sincerity, reverence and solemnity and so great a distance from all affectation, forgetting the presence of men, and as being in the immediate presence of a great and holy God, as [he] had scarcely ever known." Brainerd's long illness must have laid a heavy burden of physical and emotional strain upon the Edwards family. Elizabeth, the tenth child, was born just three weeks before he came to the house. Yet he obviously succeeded in making himself a pleasant guest and an undemanding patient. To Edwards and Jerusha, at least, his presence undoubtedly gave sweet but poignant pleasure.

Edwards' professional interest in young Brainerd was twofold. He was greatly impressed with his missionary activities among the Indians and believed that the publication of the *Memoirs* would stimulate further interest in the enterprise. In this he was not mistaken. The book was destined to be translated into many languages and to it is due, in no small degree, the efflorescence of the American missionary movement after the social upheaval caused by the War of the Revolution had subsided.

But vastly more significant to Edwards was the fact that in Brainerd he saw an accurate and vivid illustration of the kind of religion he had pleaded for in the *Religious Affections*. Alongside his wife's example he set Brainerd's as a "very lively instance of the nature of true religion." In a way the *Memoirs* constitute Edwards' fifth treatment of the revival, all the more impressive because he could now translate the abstract and impersonal terms of his previous volume into the concrete form of a thrilling and tragic personal history. To be sure, he found it necessary to criticize certain aspects of Brainerd's character and temperament. The latter was a man of moods who pendulated swiftly between elation and melancholy. Until Brainerd succeeded in transferring his attention from himself to the objective tasks and problems of his missionary career, his diary contains little else but amazing minute and repetitious descriptions of his shifting feelings. He was inclined to attribute every one of his changes of mood to the invasion or withdrawal of the Holy Spirit. Edwards did not concur: "There was undoubtedly very often some mixture of melancholy with true godly sorrow and real Christian humility; some mixture of the natural fire of youth with his holy zeal for God." Of central importance was Brainerd's total lack of a mercenary spirit. He loved God for the supreme beauty and excellency of his nature. Furthermore, the kind of self-denying, serviceable life he lived was incontrovertible evidence, in Edwards' judgment, that "there is indeed such a thing as true experimental religion arising from an immediate divine influence, supernaturally enlightening and convincing the mind and powerfully impressing, quickening, sanctifying, and governing the heart." Had Edwards needed to have his faith restored in the interpretation of religion to which he had given himself so ardently for a score of years, he could have found no better tonic than the diaries of this young missionary.

When Brainerd died he left in his host's care his manuscripts and books, among them a Hebrew lexicon which is still extant, a picturesque item in the Library of Princeton University. His Indian converts had rebound it for him, using a piece of otter skin from which they had cut the fur with stone or shell knives. They had then decorated it with irregular stripes of primitive solid color, buff, yellow, black, and red. Edwards must have counted it among his most treasured possessions.

Chapter Six

THE SACRED GADFLY OF NORTHAMPTON

Edwards was a perfectionist. "There is no man on earth that ever comes up half way to what the law of God requires of him." If he was severe in the moral demands he made upon his parishioners he was no less strict with himself. He was a hard taskmaster, ill-content with shoddy thinking and careless living. Both in his intellectual and in his moral life he held himself to severely high ideals, and other people he treated no differently. His unwillingness to be content with anything less than what he considered the best was ultimately responsible for the tragic end of his career in Northampton.

It is tempting to apply to his character the methods of interpretation some of our present-day psychologists are using. Was he hard on others in order to be lenient with himself? Did he stress reform at superficial points in order to divert attention from more deep-seated blemishes of character, tithing mint, anise, and cummin to the neglect of the weightier matters of the law? Did he threaten his people with hell-fire and sting them with rebukes because he secretly enjoyed seeing them wince? To answer such questions is far from easy, even when the individual studied is alive and is willing to disclose the hidden depths of his being. In the case of a person long since dead and for a knowledge of whom we are dependent on fugitive records the answer is far more difficult. Take, for instance, the last of the above questions. Was Edwards cruel for the sake of being cruel? Many a passage may be cited from his sermons that lends color to such a hypothesis, as certain students of abnormal psychology have pointed out. Yet much depends on the manner in which Edwards uttered these very words. A contemporary of his remarks that while preaching "he made but few motions with his hands," and that he spoke in a quiet solemn tone of voice. Obviously, then, his denunciations require a different interpretation of character from that based on similar denunciations uttered in vehement tones and with an accusing finger or a clenched hand pounding the pulpit. In one of his volumes on the revival Edwards urged his fellow ministers to have courage to disregard the critics who blamed them for declaring the truth to their people. To criticize a minister for not immediately administering comfort to those who are under awakenings "is like blaming a surgeon, because when he has begun to thrust in his lance, whereby he has already put his patient to great pain and he shrieks and cries out with anguish, he is so cruel that he will not stay his hand but goes on to thrust it in further until he comes to the core of the wound. Such a compassionate physician who as soon as the patient began to flinch should withdraw his hand and go about immediately to apply a plaster to skin over the wound and leave the core untouched would be one to heal the hurt slightly, crying peace, peace when there is no peace." Edwards himself was not squeamish nor soft-minded. He had never flinched from applying the same rigorous tests to himself that he applied to others, whereas the individual who finds pleasure in hurting people is ordinarily doing unto others as he would, but does not, do unto himself. No conclusive judgment in respect to Edwards is therefore possible. Guesses of more or less plausibility may be made and doubtless frequently will be made. But ultimately the answer, if there be an answer at all, will depend on the general impression Edwards makes upon his biographer.

"I lived with the soul of Mark Twain for a year," wrote a sensitive American biographer, "and I was morally deteriorated thereby." The present writer has lived with the soul of Jonathan Edwards a much longer period and can only report as his impression that Edwards had a rather well-balanced character and lived in wholesome adjustment to his family and a large portion of the community. He strove for perfection of knowledge, beauty, and holiness with all his heart and mind because he found them so altogether desirable. He commended them to others for the same reason. He rebuked himself as candidly and as vigorously as he did others whenever he detected any falling short. He included himself when he declared, "Let conscience be dealt with without any compliments."

His failure to maintain his position of leadership in Northampton cannot well be attributed to his failure to practice what he preached. His people discovered no hypocrisy in him. Indeed, his words were all the more telling because they throbbed with the passion of his own aspiration and self-discipline. He failed because he was unable or unwilling to think his people incapable of the same intense and ardent measures as himself.

Even during the exciting days when the revival was at its height, not all of the members of the congregation had been able to keep up the pace he set. Once the emotional pressure was relaxed they reverted to paths of less resistance. But Edwards did not slacken. He continued to hold before them the white light of perfection as he understood perfection.

He never ceased to inveigh against "worldliness." Excerpts from a sermon-outline, preached several years after the Great Awakening had passed, will make this clear. "Another thing that is apparently becoming customary and doubtless is very provoking to God, is pride and extravagance in apparel. Not that I condemn all adorning the body. (Was he thinking of the "locket and chane"?) [But it] appears to be very provoking to God when persons go beyond their rank. . . . Complying with the general customs of a country in clothing is not vulgar. On the contrary, 'tis not decent to be singular. But some fashions in themselves are ill—extravagant—very costly—immodest. . . . We in this town are evidently got to a great excess. Boston is extravagant beyond London. And we, considering all things, I think beyond them. . . . I had occasion to observe the people at Portsmouth, in both congregations in that place. That is a place very much famed for politeness and is a city much like Boston in many respects. I judged the apparel of our congregation was fully as costly. Many things that might make it proper for them to go beyond us." Sentences like these, uttered with passionate earnestness, were bound to cause offense. The more his hearers agreed with his strictures the likelier they were to direct their resentment against him. Even the implicit compliment to Northampton's fashionableness would not dispel the feeling of discomfort these words produced.

If by remarks of this kind Edwards tended to alienate the well-to-do, by others he offended the more shiftless as well as the more unscrupulous members of the community. He believed in the Ten Commandments and applied them to contemporary situations and to particular people. Religion might be the main business of life, but secular business and pleasure were not on that account matters of indifference. He considered "moral duties toward neighbor, vocation and family as necessary as religious duties."

"Thou shalt not steal" meant that people should

fulfill their business contracts. It meant a full and an honest day's work for a full day's wage. It meant paying their debts. It meant keeping up fences, taking "proper care to prevent their neighbor's suffering in the produce of his fields or inclosures from their cattle or other brute creatures." He denounced profiteering "when the necessity of poor indigent people is the very thing whence others take occasion of raising the price of provisions, even above the market." There must have been frequent opportunity for this practice in that economically unsettled era.

He spoke his mind about public officials who "take advantage of their authority or commission to line their own pockets with what is fraudulently taken or withheld from others." On occasion he exhibited the ingenuity indispensable to a minister who must adjust an ancient and authoritative lawbook like the Bible to the needs of his own generation. Some one objected to Edwards' denunciation of the practice of stealing fruit and produced a verse from Deuteronomy, "When thou comest into thy neighbor's vineyard, then thou mayest eat grapes to thy fill." Of course a literal following of such a precept would soon have depleted the rare and by no means luxuriant vineyards of Northampton. But, as Edwards pointed out in rebuttal, apple orchards were as plentiful in Northampton as vineyards were in the land of Canaan. So "the liberty given in this text to the children of Israel seems to be very parallel with the liberty taken among us, to take up an apple or two and eat as we are occasionally passing through a neighbor's orchard; which as our circumstances are, we may justly do, and presume we have the owner's consent."

The young people of Northampton were constantly on their pastor's mind. He thought the younger generation was going to perdition and he did not cease telling them so. He kept warning them against frolics, partly on the ground that they kept people up so late at night, "to the violation of family order" and partly because "in those towns where most frolicking is carried on there are the most frequent breakings out of gross sins, fornication in particular."

Among the many reprehensible customs he condemned very specifically was the practice of "young people of different sexes lying in bed together." He discussed the question in a sermon on a text drawn from the story of Joseph and Potiphar's wife. He spoke very plainly. The practice he referred to is known as bundling and seems to have been widespread in eighteenth-century New England as well as in certain other parts of the world. It was a device to insure privacy in courtship. Houses were small. Spare parlors where young couples could be together undisturbed by the rest of the family were rare. Sofas did not exist. Chairs were angular and hard, and sitting up late at night after the family had gone to bed was—at least in winter—chilly business or else very expensive of fuel. The custom spread of allowing young people to lie in bed together clothed and all bundled up. It was often quite open and aboveboard. As Charles Francis Adams remarks, "The very bundling was done by the hands of mothers or sisters."

According to Edwards, people made little of this practice and were ready to laugh at its being condemned. But he was doubtless right in thinking it "past all contradiction one of those things that lead and expose to sin. Experience and fact abundantly bear witness to it. It has been one main thing that has led to the growth of uncleanness in the land."

He also condemned dancing, on the ground that it tended to loose living and irreligion. Once some smart youngster apparently tried to catch him by reminding him that according to the author of Ecclesiastes "there is a time to mourn and a time to dance." But Edwards had a satisfactory interpretation of the passage and capped it with the remark: "Besides, when the wise man says, 'there is a time to dance' that does not prove that the dead of night is the time for it." He did not often allow even so slim a shaft of humor to lighten his discourses.

As guardian of public morality Edwards felt called upon to act when he was informed that "lascivious and obscene" literature was being read by certain young people of the church. The guess hazarded by Leslie Stephen that the books included some of the popular novels of the day, such as *Pamela*, no longer stands. Edwards, like most of his contemporaries, thought highly of these examples of the newly-invented art of prose fiction and seems to have been among the first on this side of the water to read the works of Samuel Richardson. Furthermore, it is extremely doubtful that any of them had come to his hand at this time, although *Pamela* had been published in England in 1740, four years before the present episode. If one must make some surmise as to the nature of the literature in question one might propose the "midwives' books" which certain young men of Northampton were known to have been surreptitiously reading "in contempt of the church."

Once satisfied of the truth of the allegations, Edwards preached a sermon denouncing the practice and invited the members of the church to stay after the service to consider what they should do in the matter. They voted to appoint a committee to act jointly with the pastor in the further investigation of the affair. When the committee met in his house Edwards read a list of names of young people in the church. At once the town was "all in a blaze," for practically all "the considerable families" in the town were represented on the list.

Edwards has been charged with lack of tact because he included on his list both those who were accused and those who were witnesses, without discriminating between the two. But it seems more likely that the real difficulty lay less in his manner of presenting the subject than in the fact that he presented at all a subject which cast reflections upon so many of the respectable people of the community. In itself this incident was hardly significant enough, as some have claimed, to account for his dismissal six years later. But it certainly alienated many of the young people and widened the gap between minister and people.

The immediate cause of Edwards' dismissal from the Northampton church was his change of opinion regarding the basis of church membership. In the early days of the Colony church membership and political privilege were linked together. In the course of time it was discovered that though citizens' rights could be inherited, piety could not. Many people of the second and the third generations claimed the rights of citizenship but could show none of the traditional evidences of religion. For several decades the problem of the relation between church and state had come to a focus at this point. The compromise of the Half-Way Covenant had been introduced to ease the situation. This was equivalent to the associate-membership of New England church life at the present time. It was intended to enable a person to secure some of the satisfactions which come from belonging to a group like a church, even though he could not conscientiously claim to have had the particular form of religious experience which the church advocated. Such a person was allowed to become a "half-way" member, receiving all the privileges of membership, including the important right to have his children baptized, with the exception of attending the Lord's Supper and of voting for church officers.

Edwards' grandfather and former colleague,

Solomon Stoddard, had been a leader among those who had gone farthest in adjusting the practice of the churches to the new social situation. His solution of the problem is clearly seen in the attitude he took toward the Lord's Supper, attendance at which, even under the conditions of the Half-Way Covenant, had been accounted the peculiar privilege of the church member. He advocated the interpretation of this sacrament as a "converting ordinance." That is to say it was not a special privilege of the member who is in good and regular standing but a means of education. He admitted to the Communion table not only those who could give assurance of having been converted, but also those who had not yet had such an experience but who nevertheless were respectable members of the community and who desired to associate themselves with the church. Christian people have never agreed as to how sharply they will draw the line between themselves and the "world." At times the line between the Christian and the non-Christian has become so dim as to be unobservable. Stoddard did not believe in exclusiveness. He himself was the man of affairs in the ministry. He was a member of the last generation of ministers who were not only the ecclesiastical but the political leaders of the community. His willingness to relax the requirements for church membership grew out of his interest in the life of the community as a whole.

In the Connecticut Valley Stoddard's new interpretation was widely followed. "It is not the custom here," Edwards had said parenthetically in his *Narrative of Surprising Conversions*, "as it is in many other churches in this country, to make a credible relation of their inward experiences the ground of admission to the Lord's Supper." Four years later he mentioned "those places where it is the manner to receive such and such only to the communion of the visible church as recommend themselves by giving a satisfying account of their inward experiences," adding an illuminating commentary: "I do not now pretend to meddle with that controversy." Obviously he had begun to have his doubts in the matter, but he was keeping them to himself until he should have time to study the problem at length. Meantime no issue arose between him and the church, for this was the period of the revival and few who presented themselves were unwilling or unable to meet the test Edwards proposed.

In order to settle the question Edwards determined to "search the scriptures and read and examine such books as were written to defend the admission of persons to the sacrament without a profession of saving faith." Among the more important of such books were two written by his grandfather. It was with a heavy heart that he found himself diverging more and more from the opinion of the man he so revered and in whose favor he was naturally prejudiced.

He was later charged with timidity for having kept his opinions to himself so long. The charge was incorrect both as to fact and as to motive. Edwards was no coward. Of course he "did not at all love openly to oppose his grandfather," as he told his wife. Nor did he enjoy fighting for the sheer joy of fighting. And he would have much preferred to avoid any possible cause of friction in the parish while the delicate matter of his salary was being adjusted. He was trying to persuade the church to pay him a fixed sum and thus do away with the annual problem of figuring out his salary in terms of the cost of living at the time, a procedure that gave the busybodies of the parish an opportunity to raise impertinent questions as to whether the minister was spending his salary wisely. It was not timidity that kept Edwards from speaking out more positively. When the right time came he was plain-spoken enough. Nor, as a matter of fact, was he altogether silent in the meantime. He spoke frankly if not frequently on the question. He discussed it not only with his wife, but with laymen and ministers both in the town and elsewhere. He brought it up for consideration at the Hampshire County Ministers meeting in 1745 and took the opportunity offered by the publication of his book on the *Religious Affections* to give an "intimation of his opinion that People may be thinking of it." By hints like this he hoped ultimately to indoctrinate the congregation with his point of view.

Probably his people did not read the section of the volume that dealt with "Professing Christians" or at least they did not think he had any intention of putting his opinion into practice. As a matter of fact he nowhere stated explicitly that he proposed to make the interpretation of religion therein depicted the official basis for judging a person's eligibility for church membership. Yet he was surprised that "he heard nothing of the people's taking notice that he differed from Mr. Stoddard."

His own mind was not fully made up even yet. He continued his study, endeavoring to keep an open mind. " 'Tis possible," he said to Mrs. Edwards, with whom he freely shared his perplexities, "I may hereafter see otherwise." Indeed, even after the controversy came to a head he still believed himself open to conviction and was ready to weigh fresh arguments on the other side. He also hoped that only such persons would actually present themselves for church membership as could make an adequate profession of faith, so that it would never become necessary for him to insist on his new position. For several years after the Great Awakening no one sought full membership in the church. But when a candidate did finally present himself in December, 1748, Edwards was forced to declare his position. In addition to the triple requirement of an orthodox knowledge of the creed, moral sincerity, and good behavior, which he agreed with the congregation were essential, he reinstated as a further requirement for church membership "a credible profession of godliness or sanctifying faith." From that moment on minister and people found themselves engaged in passionate and uninterrupted controversy for eighteen months. "The whole town was in a fermentation."

SACRED GADFLY OF NORTHAMPTON 123

Disturbing as Edwards' opinion and attitude must have been to the rank and file, it is difficult to believe that on this account alone they would have turned so violently against the minister who over a period of twenty years had brought comfort to their souls and prestige to their town. Two other factors need to be taken into consideration. The accumulating resentment which he had aroused by his incisive application of Christian ethical principles to individual and social practices of the community took this occasion to vent itself. Away with the gadfly! And at the same time Edwards became the victim of local party politics.

The party spirit in Northampton long antedated Edwards' coming there. Once in his predecessor's day the leaders of the two parties had come to blows with one another in the course of a quarrel in the church. "There has been," he wrote in 1751, "for forty or fifty years a sort of settled division of the people into two parties, somewhat like the *Court* and *Country party* in England (if I may compare small things with great). There have been some of the chief men in the town of chief authority and wealth that have been great proprietors of their lands, who have had one party with them. And the other party, which has commonly been the greatest, have been of those who have been jealous of them, apt to envy them and afraid of their having too much power and influence in town and church. This has been a foundation of innumerable contentions among the people." After the Great Awakening in 1740-42 he thought he observed an extensive subsidence of party spirit. "I suppose," he wrote to a friend, "there has been less appearance these three or four years past of that division of the town into two parties which has long been our bane, than there has been at any time during the preceding thirty years; and the people have apparently had much more caution and a greater guard on their spirit and their tongues to avoid contention and unchristian heats, in town meetings and on other occasions. And 'tis a thing greatly to be rejoiced in that the people very lately came to an agreement and final issue with respect to their grand controversy relating to their common lands, which has been above any other particular thing a source of mutual prejudices, jealousies and debates, for fifteen or sixteen years past." If Edwards' optimism did not blind him to the true state of affairs in the town, ensuing events made it clear that the peace was no more than a temporary truce. The "unchristian heats" still smoldered.

In addition to this party spirit within the town there was rivalry of a different kind in the country at large. In Boston they used to talk about "the river gods" of the western country. These were the men of wealth and ability who dominated the life of the Connecticut River Valley. One of them was the chief resident of Northampton, Colonel John Stoddard. Even before his reverend father's death he had assumed the leadership of the aristocratic minority. His position was like that of the squire of an English village. No one else in the community had as much money as he or as much influence. He owned the first teapot in Northampton and the first gold watch. Seventeen times he was elected selectman. He represented the town in the legislature, yet so even was the balance of power that his opponents were strong enough to prevent his election to office from time to time in bitterly fought contests. He was a county judge. He commanded the military operations against the French and Indians along the western frontier, a responsibility that kept him constantly busy. When he died in 1748 Edwards lost more than a shrewd counsellor and older friend and uncle. He lost his most influential supporter in the community. Had Stoddard lived, it is unlikely that Edwards would have fallen.

The next most important figure in the region was Edwards' cousin, the wealthy and domineering Israel Williams, of Hatfield, another of the "lords of the valley." With Colonel John Stoddard gone he stepped into the position of primacy. Edwards he disliked partly because of the latter's refusal to take his advice in the Breck Controversy many years before and partly because of his adherence to the Stoddard wing of the family, with whom the Williams branch seems to have been at odds both politically and domestically. Edwards was marked for punishment. His proposal to change the basis of church membership provided his opponents with the necessary excuse. Such Northampton men of the opposite party as had powers of leadership leaped into action, aided and abetted, apparently, by Israel Williams. The first formal hostile action on the part of the church was the presentation of a petition to the officers that the relation of Mr. Edwards to the church be considered at a precinct meeting. Of the eleven signers of this memorandum two had been included in the list of those accused of reading indecent books half a dozen years before, and seven of the others were in one way or another related to these two. Even a less astute man than Edwards would have noticed the connection between these two episodes.

Many people doubtless welcomed the quarrel as a means of relieving the tedium of village life. But others had an ax to grind. To the members of the party that came into power with the death of Colonel Stoddard it offered an excuse to eject a man who had been so closely associated with him. To Edwards and to many of the church people the point at issue was a matter of principle and conscience. From the beginning he had faint hope of preventing a rupture. "It is likely to issue in a separation between me and my people," he wrote to Scotland. He had seen little reason to change the opinion he expressed in college that "in husbandry, how difficult to persuade that a new way is better." His was an agricultural people accustomed for half a century to Mr. Stoddard's way of doing things. What power had logic against the inertia of custom or cool argument against the fiery vehemence of passion? Nevertheless he hoped against hope that the church might shift its attitude. And if argument and logic could have succeeded in changing the mind of his people surely Edwards would have won his case. The internal dissensions of a church are seldom illuminating, least of all those long by. The Northampton controversy is redeemed from mediocrity by the caliber of the protagonist and the brilliance, the cogency, and the cumulative power of the successive briefs he presented in his own behalf. The American legal profession is vastly the poorer for Edwards' going into the ministry rather than becoming a lawyer.

During the protracted controversy he was occasionally injudicious enough to refer to his opponents' practices and ideas in derogatory terms; "flagrant instance of injustice, absurd." Considering the strain he was under, the wonder is that he so seldom resorted to invective. And every slip of this kind he more than counterbalanced by his constant recognition that many of his opponents were acting in good faith, standing only for truth as they understood it and doing their duty. "The state of the people," he wrote to a friend in Salem, "is very unhappy. I would not speak to their disparagement. I know it is a day of great temptation with them and allowances must be made for them on many accounts." On the other hand, in page after page of brilliant pleading he parried every objection with rapier-like thrusts of his thought. Did they taunt him with having broken away from his grandfather's ways? He reminded them that he "did not settle here as a minister of Mr. Stoddard, but of Jesus Christ." He asserted his right to make up his own mind: "if I be not capable to judge for myself in these matters I am by no means fit to open the mysteries of the gospel." When they sought to entangle him in precedents he produced a list of his own and reminded them of precedent after precedent they had not stickled to disregard on other occasions. He used analogies from contemporary history, the English Test Act, for example, to illustrate his point.

The chief spokesman on the other side was his cousin Joseph Hawley, whom he describes as "a young gentleman of liberal education and notable abilities and a fluent speaker, who was high in their esteem and is become the most leading man in the town." Under normal conditions he and Edwards would have been quite congenial, for Hawley was not only an able lawyer, but one who refused to take a case if his client was dishonest. He was later to make his mark in constitutional law. He seems also to have enjoyed listening to sermons as much as Edwards enjoyed preaching them and made a practice of writing out brief outlines of the sermons he heard. He was one of the younger men in the community for whom the incipient social and religious liberalism of the day had an appeal. Edwards, in fact, attributed his opposition to his lax principles in religion. Of some importance also may have been his connection with that part of the family which seems to have had a feud with the Stoddard branch. Perhaps he blamed Edwards for the suicide of his father during the first revival. Whatever his motives, he carried the burden of the attack upon Edwards.

Four years later, when the emotions generated by the conflict had partially subsided, Joseph Hawley saw the affair in a new light and wrote Edwards a humble apology for his hasty, uncharitable and "immodest" conduct. The rather haughty tone of Edwards' lengthy letter of forgiveness shows how bitterly he still felt at the treatment he had received in Northampton; though the fact that he penned it while weak after a serious illness may account for some of its sharpness. Still troubled in conscience ten years later—after Edwards' death, in fact—Hawley took the risk of being thought "quite overrun with vapors" by causing to be published in a Boston newspaper a long public statement similar to the one he had made privately to Edwards.

Edwards' interpretation of the controversy is curious. He thought of himself as engaged in an argument with his people, and often spoke of "the grand subject of debate between us." Such was not, in fact, the case. His people were paying no attention to his arguments save when from time to time he pointed out to them that they were not acting legally. At first he was not permitted to present from the pulpit his reasons for his shift of opinion. To be sure, no one could legally stop him if he chose to do so. The New England minister was king of his pulpit. But Edwards, knowing the temper of the people and fearing lest he should "raise a tumult on that holy day," had volunteered to refrain from speaking on the subject on the Sabbath when people had to attend church, without the approval of the leaders of the church. He might have dealt with the issue at the Wednesday lecture, but he doubted whether, given the present state of mind, anyone would attend. The officers of the church, knowing his power as a public speaker, shrewdly declined to give their assent. Instead they authorized him to prepare a written explanation of his position. He did so and under great pressure produced in about six weeks a 75,000 word statement of a masterly character. Yet when this was printed not more than a score of copies found their way from the printer in Boston to the townspeople in Northampton and it is doubtful whether even these few were widely read. Edwards suspected underhanded plotting.

Meantime incessant talk was the order of the day—"a heap of unintelligibles." Committee meeting followed heated committee meeting in endless procession, committees of the church, committees of the precinct, joint committees of representatives of the people and the minister, conferences, reports, proposals, and remonstrances. Edwards was kept so busy he had to forego even his cherished correspondence with Scotch friends.

The controversy might have been quickly settled in one of three ways, by the church dismissing him out of hand, by his resigning, or by his yielding the point. The first course of action was not possible for a Congregational church. Having settled its minister with the advice of a council of neighboring Congregational churches it could not dismiss him without the approval of another council gathered for the specific purpose of passing judgment on the proposed action. It was on the question of the method of calling such a council that the discussion soon centered. The church proposed to invite only the near-by churches, claiming Congregational precedent therefor. They were as well aware as was Edwards that such a council would be a packed jury, since with few exceptions all the neighboring churches were Stoddardean. Edwards claimed the right to include on the council churches from a distance and reinforced his claim with very plausible arguments. Finally both sides agreed to call an informal council of local ministers to arbitrate the question as to whether he should be allowed "to go outside the county." Although these ministers disagreed with Edwards' position they were fair-minded enough to acknowledge his right to have a certain proportion of distant churches on the council. They also recognized his right to a fair hearing from the pulpit. With their moral reinforcement Edwards announced his decision to deliver a series of lectures on week-day afternoons. He was still anxious to keep the controversy out of the Sunday services. As a matter of fact, his sermons at this time, as throughout his career, are singularly free from personal allusions. No matter in what turmoil his own feelings might be, his preaching was consistently objective and self-detached. Although his opponents objected to his lecturing and few of his own people came, a large number of strangers who were in Northampton for the county court meetings attended. Even the justices adjourned court on Wednesday afternoons, despite the protest of the clerk, who was none other than Israel Williams himself.

The ministers of the neighborhood were in a ticklish situation. Most of them disliked Edwards; not merely because he was so much brainier than they, but because he had opposed the settlement of one of them and the revivalistic practices of another, and because many of them were related to the family that was heading the opposition to him. They thought his attitude toward church membership impossibly antiquated and severe. Most of them, according to Edwards, were young and headstrong. On the other hand, they were shrewd enough to recognize that the downfall of one minister, particularly one so prominent as Edwards, tended to unstabilize the position of all other ministers, themselves included. Once they almost had a panic when it seemed to them that the lay leaders of the opposition were going to plunge ahead without further regard to ecclesiastical propriety and legality. With their assistance Edwards came out victorious in both the minor points at issue. He won most of his skirmishes, in fact. Yet he lost the campaign.

A second way of ending the controversy would have been for Edwards to resign. This, indeed, he volunteered to do if the church would first agree to deal with the issue on its merits, after reading his book and hearing what he had to say from the pulpit by way of further explanation, with the additional proviso that those only be permitted to vote who had either read the book or heard him speak. As we have seen, the church declined to accept that condition, so his offer lapsed. He took very seriously his position as minister of his people. "I am the messenger of the Lord of Hosts to them," he had once said. He felt personally accountable to his God for the welfare of their souls. Particularly when, as he believed, their minds were darkened was it his duty to try to enlighten them. That is why he stayed and that is why he insisted on their giving him a hearing; for how can a minister fulfill his manifest duty of teaching if the people refuse to listen? He loved them, too, and was well nigh heart-broken by their treatment of him.

He had, furthermore, his own future to think about. Some of his opponents charged him with being concerned only to save his reputation and his pay. They misjudged the caliber of the man, though he frankly acknowledged that among his reasons for insisting that his dismissal be carried out in good and regular order was the importance to himself of a fair statement of the real issue by the council of dismission.

His situation may be described in his own words: "The removal of a minister from his people ordinarily lays him under great disadvantages and commonly hurts his reputation though indeed he be not to blame. There is left on the minds of the world some suspicion, whether something or other blameworthy or unhappy in him, his temper or conduct, was not the cause. People therefore are generally not so willing to employ such removed ministers." So he wanted a council which should explicitly declare "whether it is for anything blameworthy and scandalous in the pastor which renders him unfit for the ministry? . . . How far he has conducted himself well and treated his people justly? And how far they can recommend him as fit to be employed elsewhere in the work of the ministry?" There is something pathetic in the spectacle of America's premier theologian having to take measures to defend himself against the breath of scandal when he should be "cast on the wide world."

A third way of settling the controversy would have been for Edwards to act in a representative rather than an individual capacity, acceding to the obvious wishes of the majority despite his own scruples. Leaders have often so interpreted their function and done things with and for the group in a delegated capacity which privately they did not at all approve. But Edwards could accept no such compromise. He could see no reason "why Christ's ministers should, by resting in a partial reformation, lay a foundation for a new struggle and an uncomfortable labor and conflict in some future generation." To him the suggestion that he make no move in which he could not carry his followers along with him smacked of hypocrisy. The very qualities of mind that made him the intellectual leader of individuals here and there unfitted him for the personal leadership of a specific limited group. And yet, as often happens in cases of this kind, the standards he so intransigently upheld soon became widely adopted. The blood of the martyrs is the seed of the church.

When finally the Council met it recommended to the church by a majority of one, and over the protests of a minority which advocated less haste, that the pastoral relationship be dissolved. The two parties to the controversy were of such diametrically opposed opinions that no compromise was deemed feasible. But at the same time the Council gave Edwards the clean bill of health he had fought for. "Although we have heard of some stories spread abroad reflecting upon Mr. Edwards' sincerity with regard to the change of his sentiments about the qualifications for full communion, yet we have received full satisfaction that they are false and groundless; and although we do not all of us agree with Mr. Edwards in our sentiments upon the point yet we have abundant reason to believe that he took much pains to get light in that matter and that he is uprightly following the dictates of his own conscience, and with great pleasure reflect upon the Christian spirit and temper he has discovered in the unhappy controversy subsisting among them, and think ourselves bound to testify our full charity towards him and recommend him to any church or people agreeing with him in sentiments as a person eminently qualified for the work of the Gospel ministry."

When, on June 22, 1750, the question was put to the church as to whether they approved the Council's recommendation that Edwards be dismissed "their arms flew up, as if they went with springs." The vote was 200 to 20. The friendly and devoted minority insisted that it was his duty to lead them in the formation of a new church. This proposal was at first interpreted by the majority party as a plot to reintroduce Edwards as minister of the town church. Bitter and groundless charges were hurled against him. Edwards wisely resisted this friendly pressure, though it touched him deeply.

His was an embarrassing situation. Having no place to go, he remained perforce in Northampton. For a long time the church failed to secure his successor. In the ensuing three years at least two men declined the call. Meanwhile supply preachers filled the pulpit and occasionally, when no one else could be found, the committee turned to Edwards. At least a dozen times he accepted their reluctant invitation, but his last official discourse as minister of the church was his farewell sermon delivered a fortnight after the vote of dismission.

"It was three and twenty years the 15th day of last February," said Edwards, occupying the pulpit for the last time as minister of the church, "since I have labored in the work of the ministry, in the relation of a pastor to this church and congregation. And though my strength has been weakness, having always labored under great infirmity of body, beside my insufficiency for so great a charge in other respects, yet I have not spared my feeble strength, but have exerted it for the good of your souls. I have spent the prime of my life and strength in labors for your eternal welfare. You are my witnesses that what strength I have had I have not neglected in idleness, nor laid out in prosecuting worldly schemes and managing temporal affairs for the advancement of my outward estate and aggrandizing myself and family, but have given myself to the work of the ministry, laboring in it night and day, rising early and applying myself to this great business to which Christ has appointed me."

He singled out for specific mention various groups in the congregation and addressed a word of counsel and warning to the children, the youth, the unconverted, those "under some awakenings" and the "professors of godliness." He cautioned those who had adhered to him in the controversy to watch over their spirits lest they become embittered and vindictive toward the members of the majority party of the church. "Now I must bid you farewell. I must leave you in the hands of God. I can do no more than pray for you."

The main issue between himself and his people remained unsettled. His dismissal had solved the practical problem arising from the irreconcilability of their respective views, but it had not settled the question as to whose views were right. So far as this life was concerned, it could not be settled.

There was no court of higher appeal. But, said Edwards "it must have another decision at that great day, which certainly will come, when you and I shall meet together before the great judgment seat." To that judgment Edwards looked forward with the quiet confidence of a mind which had sought the truth in all sincerity and found it, and with the calm assurance of a conscience which had not counted the cost.

Chapter Seven

EXILE

"I am now thrown upon the wide ocean of the world and know not what will become of me and my numerous family." For a protracted and agonizing interval no opening for work appeared. After six unhappy months of waiting Edwards received a call to become the minister of the little church at Stockbridge in the Berkshires and missionary to the Indians located there. A trial sojourn of some months, during which he preached both to the English and the Indians, decided him in favor of the invitation. With the coming of summer he moved his goods and family up into the hills. Soon he was able to report: "My wife and children are well pleased with our present situation. . . . The Indians seem much pleased with my family, especially my wife." A great burden was lifted from his shoulders.

Among the motives that had led to the founding of the Plymouth and Boston Colonies was the desire to Christianize the Indians. That early ambition is still symbolized in the seal of the Commonwealth of Massachusetts, which portrays an Indian with the motto that so frequently has bannered the missionary enterprise, "Come Over and Help Us." Historians have sometimes treated this motive as of very minor importance. Just how largely it figured in the minds of the Pilgrims and Puritans cannot be ascertained. Yet the fact is that the charter of the Massachusetts Bay Colony contains this statement of purpose: "to wynn and incite the natives of the country to the knowledge and obedience of the onlie true God and Saviour of mankinde; and this Christian faith, which is our royall intentions and the adventurers' free profession, is the principall ende of this plantation." The Colony had scarcely taken root in New England when it gave substance to its faith by setting aside an appropriation for the evangelization of the Indians. The minutes of the first meeting of the Board of Trustees of Yale College show that even at the beginning of the eighteenth century many Colonists still cherished the original ambition "to plant and under ye Divine blessing to propagate in this Wilderness the blessed Reformed Protestant Religion in ye purity of its Order and Worship not only to their posterity but also to the barbarous nations," etc. A deep-seated missionary motive lay back of the founding of New England which persisted through many a generation. It was reinforced by the Great Awakening and gained new impetus, perspective, and vigor after the War of the Revolution.

When Edwards joined with his uncle, John Stoddard, in the project to set aside land in the Berkshires for the remnants of the Indian tribes of western Massachusettts he was acting according to the traditions of his country. He had considerable acquaintance, at least at second hand, with the Indian missionary enterprise, through his editorship of the *Memoirs* of David Brainerd. One wonders whether that book made him more eager or less eager to accept the call to Stockbridge. Brainerd's experience and his were to be as different as the temperaments of the two men themselves. Edwards' position as a missionary was an incident in a career primarily devoted to other interests. Brainerd had chosen missionary service as a vocation. Each was admirably suited to the kind of missionary work he was called on to do. Brainerd had been motor-minded; always on horseback. "I am obliged to ride four thousand miles a year." Yet this duty was also pleasure for him. "I cannot say I am weary of my hurry." Edwards was content to stay quietly at home. Muscular activity in itself had little charm for him. Brainerd had had a pioneer's lust for novelty. He had not cared to water where another had planted. He had sought virgin territory. He had craved new beginnings. Edwards was quite content to enter into another man's labors and build thereon. Brainerd had been temperamentally and physically equipped to be a frontiersman. "My diet," he had written in an account of one of his Indian sojourns, "consists mostly of hasty-pudding, boiled corn and bread baked in ashes and sometimes of a little meat and butter. My lodging is a little heap of straw, laid upon some boards, a little way from the ground, for it is a log room without any floor that I lodge in." In the course of his missionary career he had built with his own hands no less than four houses, in each of which in turn he set up bachelor quarters. It is doubtful whether Edwards could have managed, much less enjoyed, these prosaic yet fundamental details of existence. How should a man spend his day in the field, like Brainerd, "to procure something to keep his horse on in the winter," if he could not distinguish his own cattle?

Brainerd, in his lonely trips through a wilderness that was literally howling with wolves, had seen Indians quite untouched by civilization. He had observed their dances, their forest-feasts, their magic rites. Such blood-stirring scenes occurred in the depths of the woods far from Edwards' eye. "The Indians at Stockbridge were not altogether uncultivated." It was well for him that he never had occasion to remark with Brainerd the "prodigiousness of civilization as it appears when a person is observed to acquire it piecemeal."

Though their temperaments and their experience as missionaries stand in such sharp contrast, Edwards and Brainerd agreed in their theory of missions, as they did in their understanding of religion. To both of them to Christianize meant to civilize. They could not conceive of an Indian accepting the Englishman's God without at the time accepting the Englishman's manners and customs. Yet Edwards, like Brainerd, was not satisfied to identify Christianity with civilization. Eager as he was to do everything possible "to change the taste of Indians and to bring them off their barbarism and brutality to a relish for those things which belong to civilization and refinement," he did not believe their development should pause at this point. Religion is more than culture. He sought to create a tenderness of Christian conscience which should make his converts sensitive to the evils of the very civilization they had embraced. There is an unforgetable sentence in Brainerd's *Memoirs*: "The dark places of the earth are full of the habitations of cruelty." But so are the places lighted by the lamps of culture. Then as in later times a missionary found himself handicapped by the hiatus which his congregations perceived between the ideal he preached and the practices of the people from whom he came. "The poor savage Americans are mere babes and fools (if I may so speak) as to proficiency in wickedness in comparison of multitudes that the Christian world throngs with." From civilized men, for instance, the Indians had learned their "darling vice," drunkenness. To an Indian who objected to Christianity on the ground that Christians, too, get drunk, Brainerd had retorted, "You have never seen me drunk, have you?" Edwards had not been long in Stockbridge before he likewise had an opportunity to set over against the behavior of his thieving and cheating countrymen a similar example of Christian integrity that won the Indians to him.

Like Indians on every other American reservation since their time the Stockbridge Indians were the victims of shameless exploitation on the part of unscrupulous white men. When Stockbridge was founded in 1735 a sixtieth part of the land had been set aside for the first missionary, a similar portion for the missionary teacher, and four other equal lots for four English families. One of the latter had been taken up by Ephraim Williams, a member of the family which had participated so vigorously in the successful attempt to drive Edwards out of Northampton. As a resident of Stockbridge Ephraim Williams bought and sold lands in western Massachusetts, conducted a mercantile business, and secured increasing control of the affairs of the station. By the time Edwards arrived the village was engaged in a violent quarrel. On the one side were the "people on the hill," as Edwards called them: Ephraim Williams, powerful because of wealth and family position, his daughter, who was the widow of the former missionary, and an illiterate ex-military officer who conducted the school for the Mohawk Indian children with funds provided by a missionary-minded Londoner. On the other side were Timothy Woodbridge, the teacher of the Housatonnuck Indian children, the remaining white inhabitants, and the Indians, who resented both exploitation by Ephraim Williams and the incompetent, as well as irregular, schooling of Captain Kellogg.

For some time Edwards maintained a position of neutrality. But matters grew worse. The Williamses proposed to parcel out all the positions at the station to members of the family: the agency to one, the female boarding-school to another, the auditorship to a third. Elisha Williams, Ephraim's nephew and Edwards' tutor at Weathersfield, while visiting England had himself elected a member of the board that controlled the mission and aided and abetted these schemes. At last Edwards could stand such nepotism and graft no longer. He spoke out. At once he became the target of a virulent and crafty attack. He proposed an impartial investigation, suggesting that some disinterested trustees be appointed to live in Stockbridge where they could exercise a more immediate supervision than it was possible either for the Society in London for Propagating the Gospel in New England or even for its commissioners in Boston to give. To his delight a man was selected who had frequently expressed his confidence in Edwards. But hardly had this gentleman reached Stockbridge than he married Ephraim Williams' daughter. In no time he was as hostile to Edwards as were the other members of the family. Edwards was surprised and bitterly disappointed. The family now banded together to oust him. They lobbied at the General Court. "Captain Ephraim," so Edwards wrote to his brother-in-law in Northampton, "is in Concord constantly busy with the representatives with his lime-juice, punch, and wine." They sought the aid of influential men like Sir William Pepperell. Edwards countered by a barrage of letters to Sir William and other friends and officials, describing the situation in straightforward and convincing terms. So much confidence did people have in his integrity that his letters counted more than the personal presence of his opponents. Opinion began to turn against the Williams group. One morning, in desperation, Ephraim Williams got up early and went from home to home offering to buy the property for cash if he could have it at once. In this way he almost succeeded in securing control of the village. But the scheme fell through and he was glad to agree with his neighbors in attributing its conception to a fit of temporary insanity. Thwarted at every point, he soon sold his property to his eldest son and left the place.

For over two years Edwards had been the leader of the attack against his acquisitive neighbors and distant relatives. He won a complete victory. His persuasiveness and aggressiveness, reinforced by his reputation for integrity, saved the mission from further exploitation. The quiet scholar had again made it clear that the Gospel of Christ had implications for the social order as well as for the individual soul. Ultimately he was himself given charge of the mission station, its funds, and its staff.

Edwards had looked forward to his ministry at Stockbridge as a time of peace. To be sure, he did not mind a fight, if the cause was a good one. But controversy was distracting and he wanted to write. Not for some time, however, was he to recover his serenity of mind. His financial situation worried him. His salary came to him from three sources: the church, the Society in London for Propagating the Gospel in New England, and the provincial government. The total amount, however, proved quite inadequate to his needs. Out of it he had to pay not only his living expenses, but the cost of moving to Stockbridge. He had to purchase a house and lot and build an addition to the house. Two of his daughters had been married just before he left Northampton; now it was Esther's turn. The Stockbridge parsonage was prepared for the great event. Her husband was the brilliant second president of Princeton, Aaron Burr. A sigh of relief must have escaped Edwards at the conclusion of the ceremony. There would be no marriageable daughters about the house for some time to come.

Moving, buying a house, and woodland for fuel, marrying off daughters—all on a considerably decreased salary—it was no wonder the Edwards family went into debt. Even the considerable sum contributed by his friends in Scotland when they learned of his dismissal was insufficient to keep his balance favorable. In a pinch like this everyone turned to and helped. The children occupied their leisure in embroidering and making lace. They tamboured. They made fans and sold them in Boston. Edwards economized by using odd scraps of paper for his sermons: physicians' prescriptions, marriage publishments, requests for prayer, the children's copy-books, proof sheets, title pages of books, and even the semicircular remnants of soft paper from the fan-making. But even so the family budget did not balance until at last the Northampton place was sold.

To add to his cares his wife became dangerously

ill and her life was despaired of. Betty, the five-year-old daughter, was unwell most of one winter. Others of the family fell ill too. Finally Edwards himself succumbed to an attack of "ague and fever"—his longest and most tedious illness—that lasted for over six months and left him emaciated and enfeebled. The rumor even got abroad that he had died of these "fits."

In spite of all these distractions, however, he was able to give his attention most fruitfully to a problem that deeply interested him. Among the fascinating letters in his voluminous correspondence is one addressed to his friend, Sir William Pepperell, in which "with particularity and minuteness" he outlined his educational program for the mission. He proposed that the pupils at Stockbridge should not "learn without understanding," and advocated a method of instruction that should be "free from the gross defects of the ordinary method of teaching among the English." He aimed to "beget an early taste for knowledge and a regularly increasing appetite for it." The test of education is its ability to arouse in the pupil the joy of learning for learning's sake. To be sure, in the case of children as of adults appeal might be made to certain extrinsic motives to supplement their unmercenary love of knowledge. Let there be occasional public examinations in the school. Invite the trustees, neighboring ministers, gentlemen and ladies, and the chiefs of the Indians. Have spelling-bees and oral competitive examinations. Offer "premiums," to the pupils that excel. This will "please Indian children with but little expense." Give an exhibition of their sewing, spinning, and knitting, with rewards for excellent work. Add other prizes for those who have been truthful, diligent, well-mannered, and careful in their observance of the Sabbath. And top the affair off with an entertainment.

The obvious basis for the curriculum was a knowledge of the English language, yet this had been shamefully neglected by Edwards' unskillful and unscrupulous predecessors in the mission. He was fertile in suggestion as to how the Indian children could become proficient in English. Don't let them live at home, for there they will speak Indian and lose what they have learned in school. Acting on this very principle, Edwards sent his own son, Jonathan, to live with a tribe of the Mohawks in New York State so that he might learn their language and later become a missionary to the Indians. Either place Indian children out in "good English families, one at a place," to learn English before they are enrolled in the school, he counseled, or else provide a boarding-school for them. A tentative experiment had already been made in the latter direction, and Edwards was eager to see it continued and enlarged. He looked forward with keen anticipation to being able to stamp his new project with form and character, both by the selection of the right sort of woman to help with the school and by the wise choice of a curriculum.

A great deal was to be made of singing. Like

Edwards himself, "the Indians love to sing." He could think of no course more effective than singing to promote "the great end in view, of leading them to renounce the coarseness and filth and degradation of savage life for cleanliness, refinement and good morals." In addition to singing and reading, emphasis should be placed on the other two R's as well as on geography and history; both of the latter, it should be noted, limited to biblical history and geography. And of course, the catechism. Besides their studies the children were to attend church on Sunday and daily family prayers. They were also to learn some handicraft.

Edwards had become familiar, through Brainerd's diary, with the agricultural instruction his young friend had considered as much a part of his missionary enterprise as his evangelistic or educational activity. Brainerd himself had given instruction in planting. He had helped the Indians mend their fences. He had been shrewd enough to see that part of a nomadic Indian's salvation lay in the acquisition of a farm and of the habit of industry to cultivate it, for ownership of a farm tended to prevent him from wandering about the country and enabled him to raise the necessaries and comforts of life. Edwards could not give such instruction himself, but he arranged for the services of an agricultural missionary at Stockbridge to teach the Indians the rotation of crops and methods of planting more efficacious than their own primitive way of scratching the top-soil of a meadow and dropping a few kernels of corn in little surface hills.

Schooling and study suffered interruptions. War broke out for the fourth time between the French and the British for the control of the central part of the continent. As a frontier settlement Stockbridge had its full share of danger and disaster. Edwards could not escape war's entanglements. The town was garrisoned and four soldiers were quartered at his house in February, 1755. The immediate cause of this military measure was the killing of a local English family by Indians from Canada. As Edwards wrote to one of his Scotch friends, "We are all in commotion from one end of British America to the other." Throughout his life the rattle of musketry formed a running accompaniment to everything he did. But never did war's alarums come nearer to him personally than at Stockbridge.

Like many another Englishman in America, Edwards was critical of the home government. Nothing could be more stupid, he felt, than to send over British forces to fight the Indians in America and British officers to have command of the local troops. "Let them send us arms, ammunition, money and shipping; and let New England men manage the business in their own way, who alone understand it." It was not long before the British were to discover that the troops of these provinces, despite their divisions, understood how to fight not only the Indians, but also the picked troops and mercenaries of Europe.

Meanwhile Edwards was filling the interstices of his time with productive writing. Again and again he requested his friends to tell him of books or to send him books dealing with the subject he had half reluctantly laid aside in 1747 in order to edit the *Memoirs* of David Brainerd. Prior to that time he had already been reading an English author, Daniel Whitby, "who had engaged [him] pretty thoroughly in the study of the Arminian controversy and [he] had written upon it in [his] private papers." A letter of about this same time contains a self-revealing and pertinent sentence: "I have got so deep into this controversy that I am not willing to dismiss it till I know the utmost of these matters." In the course of his study he came at last to the point of projecting a book: "I don't know but I shall publish something after a while on that subject." It was not until November, 1753, however, three years after he reached Stockbridge, that he found himself free to devote consecutive and concentrated hours to the task. Then in the unbelievably brief space of four and a half months he composed the first draught of *A Careful and Strict Enquiry into the Modern Prevailing Notions of that Freedom of the Will which is Supposed to be Essential to Moral Agency, Virtue and Vice, Reward and Punishment, Praise and Blame*, a volume that rapidly went into several editions and long ranked as his greatest literary and philosophical achievement.

As in the case of most books of the day, the publication of the *Enquiry* depended upon procuring enough advance subscriptions to cover the cost of printing. The response to Edwards' circular showed how widespread and cordial a public he had won for himself. About four hundred and twenty-five copies were ordered. Of the three hundred subscribers, thirty or more were students at Yale and Princeton. A number of copies were ordered by Virginians and—thanks to the endeavors of his friendly correspondent, Dr. Erskine—forty-four orders were received from Scotland.

In the perspective of a later age the significance of this book appears considerably reduced. It gives undue prominence to the intellect and takes no account of the subconscious processes of the mind. From a genetic, evolutionary point of view it is marred by the peculiarly static quality which characterized eighteenth-century thinking. Other volumes from Edwards' pen rank higher in our estimation. Yet for more than one hundred and twenty-five years his *Freedom of the Will* was the object of frequent sharp attack and of equally vehement defense. He raised questions and suggested solutions which departed from traditional theology and so became the main center of discussion for a succession of later theologians, Hopkins, Bellamy, Emmons, West, and others—who formed the so-called Edwardean school of theology. As a masterpiece of subtle, sustained, and fearless logical argumentation it is still one of the most notable museum pieces of historical Christian thought.

To many the question of the freedom of the

will arises out of a personal moral crisis: can I get free of this vicious and perilous habit of mine? To others a social situation forces the problem on the attention: how far am I at liberty to control future possibilities of action? Sometimes the problem is primarily intellectual. Curiously enough, it was not this psychological phase of the question that attracted Edwards, though he had by no means abandoned his interest in the nature of the soul. For him, as for most of those who have dealt with the question, the problem of free-will was mainly religious. What kind of freedom can human beings have under a sovereign and omnipotent God? If none, what becomes of human responsibility and of the reputation of a Deity who damns and saves men on the basis of conduct which they engage in under his control?

A new school of religious thought was coming into existence at this time as one writer after another with increasing frequency and unanimity attacked the current Calvinistic theology. Historically known as Arminianism, it was referred to by Edwards as "the modern fashionable divinity." It was the theological expression of the dawning period of individualism and self-reliance that sought to break loose from the control of thought and practice which for centuries had been exercised jointly by church and state. To Edwards this incipient liberalism seemed to imperil the authority as well as demean the dignity of the Creator and Sustainer of the universe. With eager and daring confidence he set himself up as champion of an extreme Calvinism, proposing a thoroughgoing refutation of Arminianism. He selected the freedom of the will as the first topic for discussion, since, in his judgment, "it is easy to see how the decision of most of the points in controversy between Calvinists and Arminians depends upon the determination of this grand article concerning the freedom of the will requisite to moral agency; and that by clearing and establishing the Calvinistic doctrine in this point, the chief arguments are obviated by which Arminian doctrines in general are supported and the contrary doctrines demonstratively confirmed." In an appendix issued a few years later he reaffirmed his conviction of the fundamental importance of this theme. Until this question is settled Calvinists "will be obliged often to dodge, shuffle, hide and turn their backs; and the latter [Arminians] will have a strong fort from whence they never can be driven and weapons to use which those whom they oppose will find no shield to screen themselves from; and they will always puzzle, confound and keep under the friends of sound doctrine and glory and vaunt themselves in their advantage over them; and carry their affairs with a high hand, as they have done already for a long time past."

Indeed the book may be regarded as Edwards' sixth treatment of the revival, last in point of time but first in point of significance. In it he developed at length the principle which he believed was basic in the theory of revivalism. He wrote, therefore, from the fullness of his heart and with a deep sense of the wide-reaching significance of his task.

This apologetic interest accounts for his frequent recourse to Scripture to prove his theses, though as a matter of fact he relied less on the Bible in this book than he did in another critical volume composed three years later in defense of the doctrine of Original Sin. Throughout the first book there are constant references to the larger issues at stake. Its climax is a final statement indicative of the bearing of his conclusions upon the five main Calvinistic doctrines of divine providence, human depravity, efficacious grace, divine election, and the perseverance of the saints.

As his exposition proceeds, it becomes clear that he had an ideal of character different from that of his opponents. "To be at liberty to play the fool" seemed to him a sorry kind of freedom. He could discern no "sort of privilege or dignity in being without such a moral necessity as will make it impossible to do any other than always choose what is wisest and best." On the contrary, "the stronger the inclination is and the nearer it approaches to necessity in that respect, or to the impossibility of neglecting the virtuous act or of doing a vicious one, still the more virtuous and worthy of higher commendation [it is]. . . . The reason," he added, "why it is not dishonorable to be necessarily most holy is because holiness in itself is excellent and honorable." His lofty assertion that the free man is he who by disposition and habit cannot but choose the good may fail to stir an age like ours in which the idea of what is good is confused and uncertain and in which a fetish is made of experimentation. Yet this ideal of human behavior of which Edwards was the flaming prophet has had as its spokesmen some of the profoundest thinkers of the race.

"Some play at chess," said Emerson, between whom and Edwards appear so many unexpected similarities, "some at cards, some at the Stock Exchange. I prefer to play at Cause and Effect." Edwards, too, was impressed with the law and order exhibited by the universe. This is what he meant by necessity, the certain connection between cause and effect, the inevitability of every event's having a cause. Nothing is at random in the cosmos. There are no loose ends. If there were, not only would human character be unattainable, but the sovereignty of God as expressed in his divine foreknowledge and election would be imperiled; yes, proof of his very existence would be impossible, if one could not trust the law of cause and effect. The principle applies equally to the divine and the human realm. Edwards upheld a determinism that was thoroughly monistic, operative right through the universe.

Everything an individual does has its antecedent cause. It is fallacious to talk about undetermined, spontaneous behavior. Every act has its prior motive. Motives depend on the character of the individual. A man's disposition determines the kind of motive that appears strongest to him and so the choice he makes. Edwards interpreted "will" as this power to choose. A man's freedom consists in his power to do as he chooses. What other freedom could he want or imagine than the freedom to do as he pleases? This is what Edwards meant by the freedom of the will. Since a man is free to do as he chooses, he may be held responsible for his actions. Not in every instance, however, for sometimes he is prevented by external circumstances from doing as he pleases. He is then said, according to Edwards, to have a *natural* inability to act. On the other hand his character may be such that he prefers the bad to the good. He may then be said to have a *moral* inability to act in the right way. Yet his wrong action is his own action, the result of his own choice; so he acts freely and, if no external obstacle restrains him, may therefore be held responsible for what he does. It should be noted that this distinction between natural and moral inability, between *I can't* and *I won't*, occurred also a hundred years earlier to a certain French Calvinistic theologian at Saumur, who, like Edwards, was attempting to harmonize human freedom and responsibility with divine omnipotence. Amyrault and Edwards hit upon the same reconciling principle independently of each other. The latter did not know French.

Edwards was as interested in the nature of God as he was in the nature of man and in the present discussion the relation between the two constitutes a major part of the problem. A chief difference between God and man lies in the fact that the latter alone is subject to natural inability. So far as moral inability is concerned, God, like man, is limited. Only his moral inability is always an inability to do wrong. "The sovereignty of God is his ability and authority to do whatever pleases him." Yet "he cannot avoid being holy and good as he is."

Nevertheless, God may be said to have "the highest possible freedom . . . and he is in the highest possible respect an agent and active in the exercise of his infinite holiness though he acts therein in the highest degree necessarily." Edwards rejoiced that there is on God's part "no senseless arbitrariness. . . . To suppose the Divine Will liable to be carried hither and thither at random by the uncertain wind of blind contingence which is guided by no wisdom, no motive, no intelligent dictate whatsoever (if any such thing were possible), would certainly argue a great degree of imperfection and meanness, infinitely unworthy of the Deity." Edwards left no possible doubt of his attitude in this regard. It distinguishes him markedly from Calvin, with whom he in general so largely agreed. Calvin could not talk of God as bound; God does not act in a certain way because it is right; it is right because he acts that way. Like certain ancient Greeks, Edwards conceived of a power superior even to God, the power of wisdom and righteousness, though he himself was unaware of the parallelism. Even God himself was not free to be evil or foolish. God would not be God to him if he had to be "continually putting his system to rights as it gets out of order through the contingence of the actions of moral agents," if he had "little else to do but to mend broken links as well as he can," if he were "always exposed to an infinite number of real disappointments in his governing of the world." Rather than think of God as "liable to be wholly frustrated of his end in the creation of the world," he was willing to conceive of him as so completely in control of it as even to be the author of sin. To be sure, he "dislikes and rejects the phrase," preferring to say that God is the "permitter or not the hinderer of evil." God is the author of sin in two ways: as creator of the universe and as the sole source of moral goodness in man. Edwards' exposition of the latter aspect of the divine activity may be drawn from his *Doctrine of Original Sin Defended*, the exegetical companion-piece to his *Freedom of the Will*, wherein he presented succinctly a point of view to which he adhered throughout his life.

When God made man at first, he implanted in him two kinds of principles. There was an *inferior* kind which may be called *natural*, being the principles of mere human nature; such as self-love, with those natural appetites and passions which belong to the nature of man, in which his love to his own liberty, honor and pleasure were exercised. . . . Besides these, there were *superior* principles that were spiritual, holy and divine, summarily comprehended in divine love. These principles may in some sense be called *supernatural* . . . being such as immediately depend on man's union and communion with God's Spirit.

Apart from God, then, man cannot be good. His taste for virtue is a divine gift. It is the candle of the Lord shining in his mind. Only by the grace of God may his disposition be made favorable to goodness rather than to evil. Since his disposition controls his choices, God must be acknowledged as the author not only of human goodness, but also, by refraining from altering a person's natural taste, the author of evil.

In spite of this concession Edwards believed he had not forfeited the principle of human responsibility. Praise and blame seemed to him to attach to the nature of an act, since it is in the nature of an act rather than in its cause that the essence of virtue or viciousness lies. God is none the less praiseworthy because he acts necessarily. Nor is a man the less blameworthy if, in so far as he has an evil character, he necessarily chooses the wrong. For the quality of his acts freely yet necessarily performed an individual may be held responsible in the sight of God and man, subject not only to human praise and blame, but also to divine rewards and punishments.

The *Inquiry into the Freedom of the Will* should not be dismissed without a reference to the technique of the author's exposition. He employed all the weapons in the debater's arsenal to puncture the Arminian balloon. "By his own reasoning," he remarked ironically of a certain author, "the Doctor has cut all the sinews of his argument." And sarcastically, "these metaphysical terms are pure metaphysical sounds without any ideas whatsoever." Another fallacious chain of reasoning he dismissed crisply: "so the race is at an end, but the evader is taken in his flight." So sure did he feel of the validity of his own position, that at times he played with his opponents, making up arguments for them: "I confess it is an evasion of my own inventing and I do not know but I should wrong the Arminians in supposing that any of them would make use of it. But it being as good a one as I can invent I would observe upon it a few things."

Occasionally he let his wit have free play. Apropos of a confused statement in one of the Arminian books he was examining, he wrote caustically:

If some learned philosopher who had been abroad, in giving an account of the curious observations he had made in his travels should say, "He had been in *Terra del Fuego* and had there seen an animal which he calls by a certain name that begat and brought forth itself and yet had a sire and dam distinct from itself; that it had an appetite and was hungry before it had a being; that his master who led him and governed him at his pleasure was always governed by him and driven by him where he pleased; that when he moved he always took a step before the first step; that he went with his head first and yet always went tail foremost; and this though he had neither head nor tail," it would be no imprudence at all to tell such a traveller, though a learned man, that he himself had no notion or idea of such an animal as he gave an account of and never had nor ever would have.

He also defended himself spiritedly against the charge of obscuring the issue by resorting to metaphysics.

This is a very impertinent objection; whether it be so or not is not worthy of any dispute or controversy. If the reasoning be good it is as frivolous to inquire what science it is properly reduced to as what language it is delivered in. And for a man to go about to confute the arguments of his opponent by telling him his arguments are metaphysical would be as weak as to tell him his arguments could not be substantial because they were written in French or Latin. The question is not whether what is said be metaphysics, logic or mathematics, Latin, French, English or Mohawk. But whether the reasoning be good and the arguments truly conclusive.

In a footnote he dealt with the assertion of "a writer of the present age" who had said that those who hold the doctrine of necessity were scarcely worthy of the name of philosopher. It had started him thinking about himself and his reputation. "Whether I am worthy of the name of a philosopher or not would be a question little to the present purpose. If any and ever so many should deny it I should not think it worth while to enter into a dispute on that question." Even if he were not a philosopher—he was in a particularly humble mood when he finished his footnote—he bade his opponents look to the argument. "There is a difference between the contemptibleness of the person that argues and the inconclusiveness of the arguments he offers." As ideals for the man in search of truth he proposed the following qualities of mind, "capacity and humility and calmness of spirit and sufficient impartiality." His own practice suggests another essential quality, candor. "As to Mr. Hobbes's maintaining the same doctrine concerning necessity, I confess it happens I never read Mr. Hobbes." The basic honesty of his mind appears in his willingness to be proved wrong if truth was served thereby: "As to the arguments I have made use of, if they are quibbles they may be shown to be so; such knots are capable of being untied and the trick and cheat may be detected and plainly laid open. . . . I am willing my proofs should be thoroughly examined and if there be nothing but begging the question or mere logomachy or dispute of words . . . I shall either be ready to retract what I have urged and thank the man that has done the kind part or shall be justly exposed for my obstinacy." This had been the temper of his mind ever since his student days when he had observed that "old men seldom have any advantage of new discoveries because they are beside the way of thinking to which they have been so long used. *Resolved*, if ever I live to years, that I will be impartial to hear the reasons of all pretended discoveries and receive them if rational how long soever I have been used to another way of thinking." Said Emerson: "As soon as a man sides with his critic against himself, with joy, he is a cultivated man."

Chapter Eight

HIDDEN RIVERS

"I'm lonely—I'll make me a world," said the Creator in James Weldon Johnson's Negro sermons in verse, *God's Trombones*. Why should there be any world? is one of the daunting questions a parent early hears his inquisitive child put to him. What is life for? inquire such adults as have leisure and strength enough to do more than follow the exacting routine of their vocation. If there is any meaning in this strange experience of being alive in the vast universe that cradles our little day, we dearly need to know it. Is the ocean of our existence stagnant or may we detect a current in it? Is the flow quite accidental and variable or is it the very tide of destiny? And if this world really is *en route*, what better can we do than to travel with it? Thus perchance we may escape the imprisoning and debilitating sense of futility that haunts us. We may align ourselves with the movement of the universe and so find significance in our existence. Certainly if the game of life has a goal we do not want to be caught running in the opposite direction. What is the goal?

Everyone asks this question. Sometimes the inquiry is quite incoherent and the inquirer has not patience to wait for an answer. Occasionally the query is passionate and insistent and the solution reached serves not only the one who perceives it but many of his fellow beings who are too preoccupied or too lazy to think for themselves.

Edwards was not the first to inquire why God had made the world, or why there is a universe at all. Pick up the living strand of Christian thought at any point. The question is being asked and answered without intermission. "God did not create the world for his own sake, for he is sufficient unto himself," was the conclusion reached long ago by a cultured Athenian convert to Christianity. Why then? Why, for the sake of man, for the sake of the church! The greatest Christian thinker of the second century, Irenæus, summed up his generation's reflections in these words: "In the beginning God made Adam, not as if he were in need of man but that he might have some one on whom to bestow his benefits."

Edwards may not have been familiar with these solutions of the problem offered by the fathers of the church, for his knowledge of the history of Christian thought was narrowly limited. But he was familiar with similar answers in the thought of his time, and though he pronounced them all inadequate, he did not abandon the attempt to find a better one. The problem haunted him as it haunts our own generation two centuries after his death.

Edwards' college notes contain several hints of

his own answer, but like those hidden rivers in Greece that disappear in caves or *katavorthræ* to emerge miles away in lower country, so these thoughts remained dormant in his mind until the opportunity came to him in his early fifties to develop and systematize them. The raw material of his thought he hammered into shape on the anvil of the minds of two of his friends. Remote as Stockbridge was, it was still within visiting distance of his most intimate acquaintances. We are indebted to the diary of one of them, Samuel Hopkins, for our information about the memorable companionship these three men enjoyed. "August 30 (1754) Rode with Mr. Bellamy yesterday to Stockbridge," is a typical entry.

At the time of his visits to Edwards at Stockbridge Samuel Hopkins was minister of the small frontier parish of Great Barrington, seven miles south in the Berkshire Hills. He was the youngest of the group. After Edwards' death he became his literary executor, preparing a number of manuscripts for publication and at Mrs. Edwards' request writing Edwards' *Memoirs*, a small volume to which every subsequent biographer is vastly indebted. Hopkins, a farmer's son and slow to develop, somehow escaped the infection of Whitefield's evangelism while at Yale. Just before his graduation in 1741, at the age of twenty, he heard Edwards preach at New Haven. So profoundly was he impressed that he shifted his plans in order to "go and live with Mr. Edwards" and study for the ministry privately under him. Theological schools were less common then than now. Temperamentally of a somewhat melancholy caste of mind, disappointed at finding on his arrival in Northampton three months later that Edwards was absent on a preaching tour—this was the time of the Great Awakening—and feeling rather homesick at being for the first time in his life an eighty-mile horseback ride from his home in Waterbury, Connecticut, young Hopkins found in the "mothering" which Mrs. Edwards gave him one of the unforgetable experiences of his life. "She knew the heart of a stranger," he said of her many years later.

Hopkins felt at home at Stockbridge. He had often preached to the Indians under Edwards' predecessor, the earnest and faithful but somewhat stupid Reverend John Sergeant. In fact, at the latter's death he had declined an invitation to succeed him, recommending Edwards instead. With the latter so near by he frequently trotted up the river to sit in his study, his gigantic frame sprawled in a Windsor chair, a bear of a man, but a bear with brains and with an intense affection and admiration for his friend and teacher.

Less frequently another chair was occupied by Joseph Bellamy, for Bethlehem, Connecticut, where he was minister, was farther away. Bellamy, too, had lived with Edwards in Northampton as a student. Although he had been at Bethlehem, his first and only charge, scarcely a dozen years, he was already becoming known as the leading preacher of the western country. Few could equal him in the graphic and dramatic qualities of his preaching, or match his rich and varied voice; few had their knowledge so at their tongue's end. Possessed of an open-hearted expansive disposition, he took a place among people which was inaccessible both to the diffident Hopkins and to the shy Edwards. Resourceful in conversation, ready of wit and sarcastic of tongue, unashamed of strong prejudices and decided of opinion, he acquired a personal popularity quite apart from the fame which his writings and preaching brought him. A lawyer friend once said of him, "his knowledge of men seems almost next to unerring." He knew how to handle people. He even knew how to handle church rows and was often called in to smooth troubled waters, though the quarrel at Northampton was too aggravated even for a man with his gifts of diplomacy to smooth out. In his own church, however, Bellamy suavely and tactfully succeeded in introducing the changes which cost Edwards his pulpit. In addition to running his church Bellamy owned and superintended a farm which helped out his income. From time to time he took into his household Indian boys from Edwards' school at Stockbridge, and when the peril of war was at its height he invited the Edwards family to make him a protracted visit. Edwards once wrote to his Scotch correspondent, Dr. John Erskine, that Bellamy was one of the most intimate friends he had in the world and one that he had much acquaintance with. He was probably thinking of Hopkins as another.

The two younger men looked up to Edwards as their master; he looked to them as disciples and independent critics. He wrote the preface for Bellamy's first book, *True Religion Delineated,* which was published in 1750. The three of them exchanged books and periodicals. They submitted their manuscripts to each other for criticism. Occasionally when Bellamy, on one of his rare visits, had put his horse up in the barn and entered Edwards' study to find Hopkins also there, the host must have waited patiently while they discussed their latest experiences in horticulture—Hopkins had been making some interesting experiments in grafting. Then perhaps, with Edwards still in the background, the talk would drift to politics, in which Hopkins was even more interested than in apples. When the conversation got around to the war with the French and Indians Edwards would join in. All three agreed in condemning the British government's mismanagement of the campaign. In the end the conversation would turn to the main theme that drew them together. Of one of these visits in particular Hopkins gives us a hint that is tantalizingly brief: "February 12, 1755. Mr. Bellamy came to my house last Tuesday, with whom I went to Stockbridge, and stayed there two nights and one day to hear Mr. Edwards read a treatise upon *The Last End of God in the Creation of the World.* Returned home today."

This was one of several important manuscripts which Edwards did not put into final shape for publication before the time of his death. The successive appearance in print of a number of these writings, it may be noted—the first of them seven years after he died, the most recent bearing the date of 1903—has steadily enhanced his reputation for depth, freshness and versatility of thought. Even his most intimate friends did not know his mind as fully as we do today and casual acquaintances were justified in thinking of him as interested almost solely in the Calvinistic tradition.

Particularly significant among the posthumous publications is the *Dissertation Concerning the End for Which God Created the World*, dealing as it does with a question whose fundamental importance has already been suggested. As Edwards sat in his study, quiet and erect, reading the manuscript to his two eager and sharp-minded visitors, they must have smiled in delight at the very first sentence he spoke. It was so characteristic of their friend. Edwards plunged at once into definitions. He wanted to make sure that he knew and that his listeners knew just what problem it was he proposed to elucidate. He handled concepts as scrupulously and precisely as a banker handles currency. He had seen many an argument issue in stalemate because the disputants had failed to agree on the meaning of the terms they used. Forty-six hundred words—the length of a magazine article—were not too many, he felt, to devote to an explanation of his fundamental positions. Definitions are apt to make wearisome reading even for theologians, but Edwards brightened them up with picturesque illustrations, of which a sample may be given. He wanted to distinguish between a chief and an inferior end. Two objectives may be valued for their own sakes and neither of them be subordinate to the other as an end in itself, and yet one be the inferior of the other.

Thus a man may go a journey partly to obtain the possession and enjoyment of a bride that is very dear to him and partly to gratify his curiosity in looking in a telescope or some new invented and extraordinary optic glass. [Is this an unrecognized bit of autobiography?] Both may be ends he seeks in his journey, and the one not properly subordinate or in order to another. One may not depend on another but yet the obtaining his beloved bride may be his chief end and the benefit of the optic glass his inferior end. The former may be what he sets his heart vastly most upon and so be properly the chief end of his journey.

Quite as characteristic of Edwards as this careful laying out in advance of the objectives of the discussion and even more significant was his general approach to the subject. The opening sentence of the first chapter after the introduction struck the keynote: "In the first place I would observe some things which reason seems to dictate in this matter." Not revelation first, as might have been expected, but reason. Before he turned, like a good Calvinist, to Scripture to learn what is God's chief end in the creation of the world, he tried to think it out for himself; and unlike a good Calvinist he believed that he had succeeded. Now this is the accent of modernity. It is no new accent to those who have read his psychological writings. He has been dismissed by a recent writer as an anachronism. Far from it. He was attempting to give the mind of man its due. Edwards thought for himself. To be sure, he was old-fashioned, if that is the term to use, in that he considered the old themes worth thinking about. He found himself unable to treat the subject-matter of historic Christian thought as merely mythological and irrelevant. The facts of life which Christian doctrine was an attempt to interpret were too stubborn to be jettisoned in the facile way of many of his "free-thinking" contemporaries.

The issue here is a question of fact. Modern religious liberalism has for over a century been disinclined to recognize as significant facts those exhibitions of cosmic ruthlessness, human inequality, bestiality, and misery of which the ancient doctrines of divine wrath, divine election, and divine punishment, original sin and human depravity were an interpretation. Has religious liberalism, in neglecting to give an adequate philosophy for these facts, failed where a philosophy of life has no business to fail? Has modern religion glossed over the stern facts of life with a saccharine sentimentality about the fatherhood of God? Has it taken the iron out of its ethic? Sin does not disappear just because it is not talked about or recognized. Heredity remains though we may wish that all of us started from scratch.

Edwards was one of the earliest representatives of modern-mindedness in American religion. Yet he did not choose the strategy of most of the modernists of his day. They abandoned Calvinism. They declared there was nothing in it. They buried it under the clods of their ridicule. Edwards stood by Calvinism. He sensed the reality that underlay its doctrinal superstructure. His scent for facts was too keen to allow him to follow the red herring of incipient liberalism. Was he right? Would he take the same tack today? Has the time come when the open-minded Christian must again take into account the austere realities to which Calvinism tried to do justice? Must we retrace in part the road over which liberal religion has carried the American mind farther and farther from the sober facts of life? We shall not return to Calvinism pure and simple as Karl Barth and his followers in Europe seem inclined to do. Its theory of revelation, as well as its tendency to take refuge in the mystery of paradox whenever the philosophical nut becomes too difficult to crack, are likely to prove inacceptable. But Calvinism has pointed out facts the importance of which the present generation is again coming to appreciate. Perhaps, no more than Edwards, who found himself in a situation similar to ours, shall we be much longer content with theories of life whose facility is won at the expense of their adequacy to the facts themselves.

Edwards was seeking, then, for a cosmology that should approve itself to his "naked reason." To be sure, he began with certain assumptions the validity of which he did not question. He assumed that there is a God and that God is perfect. As he phrased it early in his *Dissertation Concerning the End for Which God Created the World*, there is no "indigence, insufficiency and mutability in God. . . . He is infinitely, eternally, unchangeably and independently glorious and happy. He stands in no need of and cannot be profited by or receive anything from the creature. . . . All things else with regard to worthiness, importance and excellence are perfectly as nothing in comparison of him."

Probably at this point in the reading Hopkins interrupted to remark that Edwards had not overcome his inveterate tendency to accept certain first principles without sufficient examination of them. It was a point of criticism Hopkins had expressed before. In reply Edwards would have insisted that one cannot handle every problem in a single book. One must take some things for granted. As to the existence of God, he had long since reached a positive conclusion, driven thereto by the threefold suggestions of physics—God is space; of philosophy—God is mind; and of religious experience—God is the source of our intuitions. As to the divine perfection, have men not always equated perfection and deity? An imperfect deity would not deserve the name of God.

In his description of the nature of the divine perfection, however, Edwards departed from tradition. Unexpectedly he introduced an æsthetic element. Years earlier in college Edwards had hit upon the idea with respect to love of its "proportion,—to greater spirits more and to less, less." As was the case with so many of these early ideas, he continued to hold it throughout his life. It was a startling position to take, the more so when he applied it to his interpretation of God, and it can be explained most satisfactorily by reference to his æsthetic attitude. Christians have always magnified love, evaluating it so highly as to ascribe its origin and highest exemplification to God. But they have ordinarily thought of love—whether exercised by God or by man—as directed toward an object on account of the object's want. Love is most truly love that places its strength at the disposal of another's weakness. Love shows its true colors when it ministers to unloveliness. Edwards, on the contrary, thought of love going out to an object in proportion to the latter's loveliness. Love is attracted by merit rather than by need. At no point did he diverge farther from his Christian heritage. God was to Edwards the Supreme Connoisseur. Being perfect in knowledge and in love, he has an accurate scale of values, and proportions the outgoing of his love in accordance with the relative value of things. But what is greater or more excellent than God himself? Nothing. God knows this. He is not the victim of finite prejudice, nor is he handicapped by any lack of intelligence. "God has not forgot himself." Therefore with divine accuracy of taste and perfection of judgment God must have the highest regard for himself. Thus the first point in Edwards' cosmological speculation has a definitely æsthetic flavor. God, being the supremely great and only perfect Being in the universe, cannot, in justice to his good taste, do anything else but make *himself* his chief end.

The second step, also, depended on certain theoretical assumptions which Edwards accepted without much scrutiny. God has a purpose which may be determined from an examination of its end-results. "We may justly infer what God intends by what he actually does; because he does nothing inadvertently or without design." Now what does the "astonishing fabric of the universe" suggest in regard to the nature and purpose of God? It suggests at least that God cannot be self-contained. He is a God of boundless energy. This is one of the earliest instances of the dynamic quality of American thought which has so frequently attracted the attention of the European observer. Energy latent or dormant is no energy at all. The very essence of energy is exercise, expansion, expression. What God can do he must do, or his happiness and perfection are incomplete.

It seems a thing in itself fit, proper and desirable, that the glorious attributes of God, which consist in a sufficiency to certain acts and effects, should be exerted in the production of such effects as might manifest the infinite power, wisdom, righteousness, goodness, etc., which are in God. If the world had not been created these attributes would never have had any exercise. The power of God, which is a sufficiency in him to produce great effects, must forever have been dormant and useless as to any effect. The divine wisdom and prudence would have had no exercise in any wise contrivance, any prudent proceeding or disposal of things, for there would have been no objects of contrivance or disposal. The same might be observed of God's justice, goodness and truth.

God is not only the Supreme Connoisseur who knows the best when he sees it. He is also the supreme creative Artist who "delights in the proper expression and exercise" of his creative genius.

Edwards did not himself use the analogy of an artist as other theologians have done and as this exposition of his thought suggests. At certain points such an analogy would not have suited him at all, for an artist has to work with given materials of wood or pigment or stone and is necessarily limited by the defects of the medium he works in, whereas God, according to the Christian theology, is not handicapped by having to work with defective materials. He created the world out of nothing. But on the whole the interpretation of God in terms of the artist as connoisseur and creator is admirably suited both to elucidate Edwards' thought and to suggest its affinities. He gave his theology an æsthetic turn, prophetic of the Romantic movement which even in his day was gathering headway.

A scrutiny of the universe suggested to Edwards something further about the purpose of God. The universe contains beings who are intelligent, connoisseurs themselves within the limits of their human capacities. Finite as it is, their understanding is something which even God may desire to enjoy, for an artist loves to have his work known. "It is a thing infinitely good in itself that God's glory should be known by a glorious society of human beings." Not only does an artist desire to have his work known, he loves to have it appreciated. So God loves to have his excellency loved. Thus, in creating intelligent beings, he still makes himself his chief end, for thereby is knowledge and love of himself increased. Because of his creation of the world there is a greater amount of love and knowledge of God than would have obtained had he not created the world.

As human beings come to know God and love him they are doing exactly what God is doing and doing what God created them to do. The reason why man's chief end is to glorify God and enjoy him forever is because this is also God's own chief end. Our behavior should parallel the divine behavior. Our perfection is of the same kind as God's perfection. We coincide with the universe, we align ourselves with its dominant tendency, we obey the will of God, in so far as we live a life of contemplation of the divine excellency as well as a life of love to our fellow creatures in proportion to their excellency, potential or actual.

This exposition of Edwards' cosmological philosophy has thus far dealt with only one aspect of his thought. It now becomes necessary to examine another element which thrusts itself inharmoniously into the discussion. Hitherto he has been thinking of God in terms of analogies drawn from the human realm. The very title of his book gives the measure of his thought. God is creator.

God is to be thought of as "creating, preserving, using, disposing, changing or destroying." But alongside this frank anthropomorphizing of God another mode of interpretation finds its place. Edwards drew upon the impersonal world of nature for his analogy. He likened God to a fountain.

God is not only the artist creating a world out of nothing; he is also a spring of water that by its very nature must bubble over and increase. God cannot help expanding. His being has a tendency to spread itself. His fullness will not be contained. God is like the "root and stock of a tree" whose disposition to "diffuse and send forth its sap and life is doubtless the reason of the communication of its sap and life to its buds, leaves and fruits." Thus the world represents the bubbling-over of the divine nature. God would not be "in his most complete and glorious state without this emanation," as Edwards technically called it, "of his own infinite fullness." As from the sun comes forth light and from the fountain of water comes forth water, so from God comes forth "something of God." He communicates himself. Obviously we have here the basis of Edwards' equation of God and the general system of existence. God is the total order of things, for it has proceeded from him.

This idea harks back to his student days at Yale. Like similar statements in his college notes, it looks in the direction of pantheism. Now as a matter of historic fact, most proponents of a pantheistic cosmology have tended to minimize the significance of personality in God. Taking as the point of departure for their philosophy the facts of nature rather than of humanity, they find themselves embarrassed when they try to make room for human values in their scheme of interpretation. Not so with Edwards. His mind passed back and forth with no apparent jolt or difficulty from a pantheistic to a personalistic interpretation of God. On the one hand the world is an emanation from God. On the other hand the world is a creature of God, a divine manufacture, "a machine which God has made for his own use." Edwards perceived no incongruity between the two interpretations. It seems not to have dawned on him that there is a contradiction in speaking of God as at the same time a person and an expansive substance.

His failure to observe the patent discrepancy between these two modes of interpretation can be given a partial explanation. Edwards at least at times thought of the expansive substance of God as a spiritual fullness. "The whole of God's internal good or glory is in these three things, viz., his infinite knowledge, his infinite virtue or holiness and his infinite joy and happiness." That is to say, his substance is personalized. Perhaps his interpretation of substance in terms of energy also served to obscure the discrepancy. "God is in his own nature a perfect Act"; "in the divine essence there is no distinction of substance and act." Both substance, as he conceived it, and person exert force; both are sources of energy. Furthermore, he thought of creation as a continuous process, not just an initial single act of God. Yet, strictly speaking, the use of analogies of emanation drawn from the physical world have no place in the description of the communication of such human qualities as intelligence and love. Air may expand. Water may flow. But not knowledge and goodness. They are communicated and shared by persons. They are not self-activating.

Actually, what Edwards did was to revive and develop the pre-theological speculations of his college days in regard to the nature of God and his relation to the world while at the same time completely modifying them in the direction of his traditional theology. It remained for another American almost a century later to take the same pantheistic ideas and use them without modification to interpret his world. Emerson became frankly pantheistic. He declined to think of God as a person. "I like impersonality." Edwards found himself attracted to such speculation, but did not accept it—at least in his maturity—without so modifying it as wholly to draw its sting.

He subordinated emanation to creation. The emanation of God's fullness he interpreted as the consequence of his creative will. Though God and the world make up one system of Being in general, yet God is the head of the system and its infinite creator. Human beings considered from the point of view of the divine emanation are parts of God. Yet the reader must check himself when he begins to exclaim, here by anticipation is the doctrine of the divinity of man; here is Emerson born out of due time. Emerson inferred from this pantheistic interpretation of the relation of God to the world that humanity is deified:

> Draw, if thou canst, the mystic line
> Severing rightly his from thine,
> Which is human, which divine.

But Edwards did not draw this conclusion from his theory of divine emanation as it would seem logically he should have done. On the contrary, he never blurred the distinction between God and man. He never identified the two. God is always God and man is a worm of the ground. In so far as God takes pleasure in the love of that which is so insignificant he does so because he forsees the future perfection of the elect.

Edwards then did not succeed—who can?—in harmonizing his pantheism and his Calvinistic theism. He arbitrarily subjected the former to the latter. Theism triumphed over pantheism. Religion again took precedence over philosophy as it had done when he was choosing a career.

Before concluding the "rationalistic" first chapter of his book on *God's Chief End in the Creation of the World* Edwards endeavored to forestall certain objections. A theistic cosmology has frequently been the butt of criticism on the score of the inhuman, immoral, unethical character of its God. Edwards' particular interpretation of the character of God appears to increase rather than to diminish the difficulty of the apologist. His God is not only severe, unregardful of the rights and dignity of man, and pitiless; his God is selfish. He loves himself. He makes himself his own end in the creation of the world. He loves to be loved. Is not this selfishness par excellence? Edwards had already in college felt the force of this objection. He acknowledged that selfishness was still abhorrent to him but went on to enquire exactly what is meant by the term. For his answer he borrowed the interpretation of a contemporary English philosopher, Thomas Wollaston. According to the latter, selfishness is a disposition on the part of anyone to put himself first, or to "regard" himself as Edwards said. Such an attitude is "mean and sordid" because it sets up an individual private value above the wider social values and the needs of other people, and so fails to recognize the priority of the whole over the part. In the case of God, however, who is the author and head of the whole system of Being, there are no values or interests outside and above himself. It is quite in accordance with the nature of things for him to put himself first. He is not selfish in so regarding himself. In fact he cannot but be selfish in this sense. If this still be called selfishness, it is at least a selfishness that has no evil connotation. It might be called a true selfishness in distinction from a false selfishness which treats an individual more highly than he deserves.

Edwards attempted with varying skill to meet still other objections to his theory. It mattered little to him, however, whether or not he succeeded in making ethically palatable his interpretation of the divine nature and purpose. He was more interested in the truth of things than in their pleasantness. If the character and purpose of God do not suit our human convenience, that is too bad, but it cannot be helped. God is a matter of fact, not of fancy. There was a certain grim objectivity in the Calvinism to which Edwards gave renewed vitality, a refusal to wrench the facts to suit the theologian's private preferences, which reminds one of the temper and ambition of present-day scientists who also aim at objectivity and the avoidance of what is known as "wishful thinking."

In his first chapter Edwards insisted on forcing reason to carry him as far as it could, although he recognized the mind's inadequacy to comprehend very fully the infinitely sublime. He next turned to revelation for further light on the end for which God created the world. His conclusion was similar to the one he had already reached. One can hardly avoid the feeling that he did not so much find this conclusion in Scripture as impart it to Scripture. Nor can one escape the impression that Edwards felt himself no more, or perhaps it would be more correct to say, no less secure in the guidance God gave him through the use of his reason directly than in the guidance he gave him through the Bible. If to Edwards reason was not wholly adequate, neither was Scripture, though either of them might be trusted to give a sufficient answer to this most searching and practical question as to why there should be a world.

Chapter Nine

MINDS ACROSS THE SEA

Intellectual traffic across the Atlantic Ocean vastly increased during the half century between Edwards' birth and death. His reading list gives evidence of his own rapidly multiplying acquaintance with the theological and philosophical literature of the British Isles. Ever since his college days when he had aspired to make his mark as an intellectual force abroad, Edwards had Europe in mind. From 1743 on he was in frequent correspondence with several Scotch clergymen. During his pastorate at Northampton a number of his books were republished overseas. After his dismissal from the Northampton church he was urged to consider taking a church in Scotland, but declined on the ground that with his large family he could not risk the possible failure of his "gifts and administration" to suit a congregation there.

His mind did not work in an intellectual vacuum. He fed it with much of the important thinking of the time, devouring such books as he could lay his hands on by loan from other ministers, by purchase from his London bookseller or by exchange. "I am glad," he wrote a Scotch friend apropos of David Hume, "of an opportunity to read such corrupt books, especially when written by men of considerable genius, that I may have an idea of the notions that prevail in our nation." By force of circumstances he came to inhabit the frontier. But his mind was not on that account provincial. It reached out across the sea and moved familiarly among the thoughts of men who were ushering in the modern theological and ethical era.

At no point is his reach more evident than in his treatment of the philosophy of ethics. What is the meaning of goodness? This question he, like most students, had posed in college days. In the elaborately outlined book which he projected at that time he included a section on "The Nature of Excellency or Virtue." The brief answer he then gave he did not afterwards modify in any essential way, though he later tested his theories in the light of contemporary ethical thought, making in this connection a further study of such British philosophers as Shaftesbury, Wollaston, Francis Hutcheson, Cudworth, Hume, and others unnamed who counted among "the most considerable of late writers on morality." Hutcheson, in particular, is one of the watershed minds in the history of ethics. Indeed, modern ethics may almost be said not only to have begun, but to have long continued with him. Thus Edwards became the channel through which the new ethical insights of Great Britain were transmitted to America to yield a rich harvest in succeeding generations.

> "Beauty is truth, truth beauty,"—that is all
> Ye know on earth, and all ye need to know,

sang Keats. Beauty is Virtue, said Edwards in his *Dissertation on the Nature of True Virtue*, a companion-piece to *The End for which God Created the World*, but that is not all you need to know about it.

Throughout the course of European culture the mind of Plato has acted as a vital germ of influence, a constant ferment. The Platonic tradition, as Dean Inge calls it, has persisted as a prominent feature of the spiritual landscape of Europe and America. Occasionally the Hellenic note seems to have been struck quite spontaneously, as though an individual had himself hit upon the same golden seam of insight that Plato had earlier discovered and exhibited to the world in golden words. Oftener, perhaps, the Greek interpretation of life has passed from mind to mind and from generation to generation like the fiery Greek beacons which carried from mountain top to mountain top the news that Troy had fallen, one enlightened spirit setting another on fire. So Shaftesbury or Cudworth or Hutcheson lit the mind of Edwards. To them he owed his definition of virtue in terms of beauty. This Hellenic collocation of terms is arresting. In itself, however, it is not wholly illuminating; for what is beauty? Until the meaning of beauty is ascertained, the nature of true virtue remains obscure.

Edwards had a sensitive eye for beauty and he perceived it in odd as well as in familiar objects. It crowded in upon him everywhere; for example, "the figures on a piece of chints or brocade" are often beautiful and the "various notes of a melodious tune." The mutual agreement of the sides of an equilateral triangle is beautiful; so is "the agreement of the colors, figures, dimensions and distances of the different spots on the chessboard" and the fitting of a mortise to its tenon. A human body or countenance may be beautiful; so may a piece of skillful architecture or a complicated machine, a solar system or a tree. Even a well-ordered society is properly described as beautiful. Now all these objects seem beautiful because of the possession of a common quality. Edwards' early manuscripts contain diagrams of dots, lines, and circles to show what this quality is. It is proportionateness. Wherever there is harmony, symmetry, uniformity in the midst of variety, is beauty. Beauty is always a kind of relationship. "One alone, without any reference to any more," he asserted, cannot be beautiful. Edwards' special technical term for this agreement or harmony was "consent."

Why is it that proportion is beautiful and disproportion ugly? This inescapable question of æsthetics cannot be answered, according to Edwards, without taking into account the nature of existence itself. The fact is that "Being, if we examine narrowly, is nothing else but proportion." That is to say, no single object can exist unless its parts are held together in a mutual balance and agreement. Nor could the sum-total of objects exist unless the agreement and order among them were greater than the disorder. Orderliness, harmony, is a principle fundamental to existence. Where sufficient balance is wanting an object disintegrates. It tends to disappear.

Now according to Edwards "a state of absolute nothing is the aggregate of all the contradictions in the world." With a flash of poetical imagery such as frequently illuminated his pages he added: "when we go about to form an idea of perfect nothing . . . we must think of the same that the sleeping rocks do dream of." He believed, therefore, that "it is necessary that some Being should eternally be." But without proportion there can be no Being. And proportion is the essence of beauty. Existence as such is therefore beautiful. Beauty is a quality of the objects which constitute the world.

Edwards was obviously more interested in the metaphysical than in the psychological aspects of æsthetics. To be sure, on at least one occasion he wrote as though he believed that the human mind imposes beauty on the world. "How exceedingly apt we are," he exclaimed, "when we are sitting still and accidentally casting our eye upon some marks or spots on the floor or wall, to be ranging them into regular parcels and figures; and if we see a mark out of its place to be placing of it right by our imagination, and this even when we are meditating on something else. So we may catch ourselves at observing the rules of harmony and regularity in the careless motions of our hands or feet and when playing with our hands or walking about the room." Yet even this experience did not suggest to him that beauty is merely a particular way the mind apprehends the world. In the æsthetic experience the mind becomes aware of beauty which is already existent in the world as a characteristic of what he called "the necessary nature of things."

Edwards called attention to a further characteristic of the æsthetic moment. The mind—perhaps he should have said, his mind—is so constituted that it is affected more by a large object that is beautiful than by a smaller beautiful object. "So the beauty of the solar system more than as great and as manifold an order and uniformity in a tree." Beauty may be quantitatively measured. "The more extended or limited its system is, the more confined or extended is its beauty."

In the light of this exposition of Edwards' idea of beauty in terms of proportion and extensiveness it becomes possible to understand what he meant by virtue. With characteristic impatience of generalities, even such a glittering one as that virtue is beauty, Edwards proceeded at the very beginning of his *Dissertation* to scrutinize and analyze his Hellenic nugget of wisdom.

Virtue is beauty, we are told. Yet obviously not everything beautiful is virtuous; for instance, the beauty of such inanimate objects as a building or a rainbow.

Nor is all human beauty virtuous; for example, such physiological beauty as that of a fair countenance, a graceful motion, or a melodious tone of voice.

The beauty that is virtue is to be sought in the human mind. Yet even here a distinction needs to be made. Intellectual beauty such as the speculations of a philosopher or the projects of a statesman are hardly to be called virtuous. We must rule out beauty of the understanding.

It is in the moral realm, where praise and blame are applicable to actions, that beauty becomes goodness, which is a quality of the disposition or will. Yet not every particular habit or disposition, not one, for instance, which is operative within a limited sphere and which takes no account of the total context of the act, can be called virtuous. Edwards was emphatic on this point. "*That only*, therefore, is what I mean by true virtue, which is *that*, belonging to the *heart* of an intelligent Being, that is beautiful by a *general* beauty or beautiful in a comprehensive view as it is in itself and as related to everything that it stands in connection with." Minds constitute a system of being. When any given mind relates itself to the whole system of existing minds without discordance or limitation, that relationship is truly beautiful and wholly virtuous.

Like the perception of natural beauty, the perception of moral beauty, or virtue, is intuitive. But the two kinds of intuition should not be confused. Good taste is one thing. Moral sensitivity is another. Yet the one may have some bearing on the other. Edwards must have been thinking of his own fondness for music and his delight in the loveliness of outdoors when he spoke of the tendency the sweet harmonies of natural beauty and sound have to "enliven in [us] a sense of spiritual beauty." But, genuinely concerned as he was with character, he never allowed himself to forget the hazards that beset the lover of beauty. He was at some pains to point out the absurdity of affirming that "a disposition to approve of the harmony of good music, or the beauty of a square or equilateral triangle, is the same with true holiness or a truly virtuous disposition of mind!"

Whether or not good taste can be cultivated Edwards seems not to have considered. Apparently he agreed with Hutcheson that the Creator implants in us an internal sense by which the mind is capacitated to discern natural beauty. On the same analogy he believed that the appreciation of spiritual beauty lay beyond the power of an individual to acquire. Like a relish for God, the spiritual taste for the beauty of holiness is a divine gift. That is to say, in the last analysis, education cannot insure appreciation. There remains an elusive, uncontrollable factor which Edwards preferred to interpret not as chance, but as the arbitrary will of God.

Ossa piled on Pelion towers over the horizon of European culture. But above them rises Calvary piled on Sinai. To both mountain ranges of the spirit Edwards was accustomed to lift up his eyes for help. Greece has given us virtue in terms of beauty; Judea, virtue in terms of love. "Love is the grand Christian virtue." Yet the latter statement, like its fellow-proposition from Plato, Edwards felt also needed analysis. The conclusion he reached was that the Christian and the Hellenic propositions concerning the nature of true virtue meant the same thing.

Edwards did not linger long to point out that by love he did not mean sexuality. Nor did he need more than a parenthesis to dismiss the interpretation of love as directed toward any other objects than intelligent beings. One does not love things. One likes things. One loves persons, or intelligent beings, as Edwards preferred to say.

By love to a person Edwards meant a finding of pleasure in that person's happiness as well as an inclination to promote his well-being and desires. We may delight in another for his beauty, we may also do good to another, not because he is beautiful but just because he is, because he exists. The former attitude Edwards, using a nomenclature of long standing with him and common among ethical philosophers, called love of complacence; the latter, which is "the main thing," love of benevolence.

Like beauty, love has its gradations. Its greatness is measured not by its intensity but by the size, that is to say, the spiritual dimension, of its object. The greater the degree of the object's existence, the greater the benevolence which is directed to it. Now there is one Being and but one Being who is the greatest Being, namely God, whose "Beauty is as it were the sum and comprehension of all existence and excellence." To the individual, therefore, whose mental faculties are able to discern these two facts about God, God is the supreme object of his benevolent love. Virtue is in final analysis love of God.

Is there, then, no such thing as a Christian love to one's fellows? Certainly there is, said Edwards, but only under Christian conditions. Love for a particular human being is virtuous in so far as it grows out of a love to Being in general, on whom every particular being depends and from whom each is derived. How may this be ascertained? Love to the creature may be recognized as arising from love to God when it coincides with God's purpose for that creature. When, in other words, it seeks to promote that creature's "knowledge or view of God's glory and beauty, its union with God and conformity to him, love to him and joy in him."

Fortified with an understanding of the nature of true virtue, Edwards was prepared to examine and evaluate the pressing throng of contemporary substitutes for a theological ethic. As has already been indicated, he had to turn to Europe for any fresh ethical suggestion. In America no one besides himself was interested or competent enough to produce much that was novel. Abroad Edwards encountered a variety of efforts to work out a naturalistic basis for the ethical life. Hobbes had found what he thought was the explanation of human conduct in the principle of self-interest. Shaftesbury, and after him, Francis Hutcheson, opposed him with the opposite principle of altruism. Edwards' attitude toward these rival theories was one of great hospitality. He acknowledged the important part they severally played in the interpretation of the moral life. He was willing to agree that most human behavior could be explained in terms of self-love or of altruism—depending on the definition of those terms. He granted that natural conscience is quite able to form true moral judgments and that the instincts of pity and gratitude will account for a host of actions that are in themselves indistinguishable from the acts of true love. Why not? Has not God so constituted us that these natural principles should be exceedingly useful to society and tend to the good of mankind? For example, self-interest will prompt many a man to avoid vices like drunkenness, gluttony, sottishness, cowardice, sloth, and niggardliness because such behavior lowers his social standing. He will stand by his party and take care of his family in order to maintain his prestige in the community. "There are no particular moral virtues whatsoever but what in some or other of these ways and most of them in several of these ways come to have some kind of approbation from self-love."

Idealistic Edwards could be and he could soar to dizzy heights of idealism on the firm but fragile wings of speculation. Yet he never lost touch with the practical interests and everyday relationships of life. No one who has read his sermons can forget that. His mind was equally facile in its dealings with the abstract and the concrete. He knew how to approach people on the level of their moral sensitiveness. So it was that when dealing with men on the natural level he treated them quite often as though he had never thought or written about the drawing power of love and beauty. He appealed to their self-interest. He threatened them. He scared them. Nevertheless, effective as these natural incentives were, he believed none of them could stand comparison with the sanctions that lead to true virtue. Both because of its practical consequences and because of its metaphysical and scriptural correctness Edwards embraced the theory of virtue as consisting in and based on love to God.

The advantages he felt were all on the side of a theological ethic. "A regard to Deity," he pointed out, "is the most important part of morality" for two most significant reasons. It gives not only an adequate basis for judging what is good but also an adequate incentive to act on such judgment. It provides both standard and sanction. The trouble with a secular ethics, whether of an altruistic or a self-regarding stripe, is first of all the narrowness of its range. It centers its attention on something less than the whole. Even "if a man's affection take in half a dozen more and his regards extend so far beyond his own single person as to take in his children and family, or if it reaches further still to a longer circle but falls infinitely short of the universal system and is exclusive of Being in general, his private affection exposes him to pursue the interest of its particular object in opposition to general existence." For illustration of his thesis Edwards referred to party loyalty and patriotism: "Among the Romans love to their country was the highest virtue, though this affection of theirs, so much extolled among them, was employed as it were for the destruction of the rest of the world of mankind." Nothing less than the all-embracing comprehensiveness of Christian love or virtue will prevent a man from becoming a greater enemy to the universal system in proportion as he becomes more virtuous within the constricted area of his private loyalty. The better he is within the narrow circle of his self-love the worse he is from the point of view of the whole. Love to God stands as a permanent corrective to limited and self-destructive affections. Only *sub specie æternitatis* does a man acquire ethical perspective. Though in Edwards the discussion of this point is somewhat abstract, it prompted his disciple, Samuel Hopkins, to rephrase it more concretely in one of the most searching and elevated accounts of unselfishness ever written, *The Nature of True Holiness*.

Love to God also provides a dynamic superior to that of secular ethics. What is the best that may be expected from a natural conscience, granted that it is normal, that is to say, "Well-informed and not stupified by sensuality"? At best it can *approve* true virtue. A man's moral judgment may quite clearly discern the right. But it lacks power to do the right. That is because "it takes no sweetness in benevolence to Being in general." But the sight of the beauty of Being in general has a tug that pulls a man to it. It draws a person out of himself. It elicits from him a dynamic, disinterested response. Nothing short of a haunting, fascinating, adorable vision of the whole in all its beauty can give a man the energy necessary to the achievement of the ideal by the service of the unideal.

So, to quote the concluding words of Edwards' own grand summary: "It may be asserted in general that nothing is of the nature of true virtue in which God is not the *first* and the *last*; or which with regard to their exercises in general have not their first foundation and source in apprehensions of God's supreme dignity and glory and in answerable esteem and love of him and have not respect to God as the supreme end." Thus Edwards gave his ethics a religious basis. He declined to align himself with those of his contemporaries who were attempting to divorce ethics from religion and make the former self-sufficient and autonomous. God, he declared, is both the goal and the sanction of true virtue.

Chapter Ten

AT PRINCETON

With the decrease of danger from the war, Edwards, now as far as he could tell permanently established at Stockbridge, was able to give himself wholeheartedly to a routine that was very attractive to him. He preached four times on Sunday, twice to the English and twice, with the help of an interpreter, to the Indians. But often he used old sermons for the first group and the material for the second had to be extremely simple. For the rest he could sit before his curious hexagonal desk swinging on its pivot, write the books that have just been described, and dream of other volumes for the future. He had many literary projects in hand. On some of them he had made great progress. One to which he often turned with "profit and entertainment" was a comparison of the Old and New Testaments, which promised to be a thoroughgoing commentary on the Bible. Even more elaborate and original was a treatise on theology. He proposed to use the historical approach and to consider the major doctrines of Christianity in their specific relation to the doctrine of salvation. He had first projected this book in an extensive series of sermons twenty years before and had now taken it up again with a view to publication when, with tragic suddenness, his days of study and writing were brought to an end. Just two days before the 1757 Commencement of the College of New Jersey, the forty-year-old President, Aaron Burr, his son-in-law, died. Within less than a week the trustees, assembled for the exercises, elected Edwards as his successor. This was a shrewd move on their part. Doubtless some of them agreed with certain critics of their action that "Edwards was rather adapted to a recluse serious contemplative life than to the labors of a college and that the volatility of 100 youths would disturb his calm quiet and make him unhappy." Nevertheless, Edwards' reputation had grown so fast in spite of the debacle at Northampton that they were well aware of the prestige he would bring to the institution. Furthermore, he could not but be a tremendous intellectual force in the student body. Academic institutions have probably suffered more from an over-emphasis on the administrative powers of their presidents than from an over-emphasis on their scholarship. The Princeton trustees knew what they were about. But Edwards received the notice of his election with a sinking heart. It is doubtful whether any of the many difficult decisions he had had to make cost him as much agony of spirit as did this one.

He was thoroughly acquainted with the college, now entering the second decade of its history. At one time Governor Belcher of New Jersey had consulted him about the revision of its charter and received from him a number of "kind hints." Just before the storm broke in Northampton, Burr, who was at the time minister of the Newark church, had urged him to "run away from these difficulties and accept the place of the President of New Jersey College." He may also have known that Princeton had had an eye on him for the professorship of divinity and that only a lack of funds had prevented them from calling him. Most of the men who founded the college were Yale alumni, many of them his friends. Shortly after settling in Stockbridge he had attended the Princeton commencement and preached at the meeting of the New York Synod of the Presbyterian churches there assembled. So he knew the college at first hand as an institution that "is in flourishing circumstances, increases apace and is happily regulated." He heartily approved of its policies and its aim to supply the awakened and multiplying churches with educated leaders so that they would not need to rely on a theologically illiterate ministry of untrained laymen. Again and again he had taken delight in writing his Scotch friends about the progress of "the young daughter of the Church of Scotland," as Princeton was called. Many of them were keenly interested in the college, for Scotland had contributed most of the money for the building of Nassau Hall. At the time of its erection this building, according to Esther Edwards Burr, was "the most commodious of any of the Colleges as well as much the largest building of any upon the Continent. There is something very striking in it and a grandure and yet a simplicity that can't well be expressed." The building was something for the small college to grow up to. Founded in 1747, eleven years before, it now had an enrollment of approximately seventy students and a faculty consisting of a president and a couple of tutors. Yet it had men of large vision and affluence on its board and an alluring future before it.

A couple of summers previously, his daughter, Esther, had sailed up the Hudson from New York in a sloop and crossed the hills in a wagon to visit her family at Stockbridge, bringing with her her baby, Aaron, who was destined later to achieve such a notorious place in American history. The visit was not altogether a success, for Mrs. Edwards had to leave almost at once for Northampton to be with another daughter, Mary, who was expecting a baby. "You can't conceive," Esther wrote to her intimate friend in Boston, "how everything alters upon my mother going away. All is dark as Egypt." Furthermore, Esther was "scared out of her wits" by hostile Indians in the vicinity. "I want to be made willing to die in any way God pleases," she put in her diary, "but I am not willing to be butchered by a barbarous enemy nor cant make myself willing." Nevertheless, there was time for much talk in the family. "Last evening I had some free discourse with my Father on the great things that concern my best interest. I opened my difficulties to him very freely and he as freely advised and directed. The conversation has removed some distressing doubts that discouraged me much in my Christian welfare. He gave me some excellent directions to be observed in secret yt tend to keep the soul near to God as well as others to be observed in a more publick way. . . . O what a mercy yt I have such a Father!—such a guide!" It may well be imagined that many things this vivacious daughter told her father about Princeton made him thankful he was not its president. It was "company come and go, come and go continually it is Rap, Rap, is the President at home all this day." There were problems of discipline, too, that Edwards had been quite free from for some years now. The student who failed to observe the rule requiring him to keep his hat off when he approached within ten rods of the president or within five rods of a tutor, was a simple delinquent compared with some of the offenders.

Only a few months before his death Burr himself had paid his father-in-law a brief visit. Edwards admired him greatly, a "little small one as to body," according to a contemporary description, "but of great and well improved mind," a first-rate scholar, sociable, witty, pious. Doubtless the enthusiastic young president told Edwards of the recent bequest to the college of an electrical machine and globes which Benjamin Franklin had given to Governor Belcher. Edwards shrank from becoming the successor of a man who was so able an executive, so competent a teacher, and so winning a leader.

On the other hand, he had long been identified with educational affairs. When he was a tutor at Yale, the college was without a president for two years and Edwards, together with two other young tutors, had done all the teaching and run the college, too. As a minister the educational problems of the community and the church were constantly on his mind. The minister of a New England church had the double title of Pastor and Teacher, and Edwards took seriously the religious education of his parishioners. At Stockbridge the educational problems were more elementary, to be sure, but he had shown himself eager to solve them and ready to try out new methods.

He was in a quandary about the call to the presidency of the college. With charming candor he explained his dilemma in a long letter to the Princeton trustees. He mentioned his defects in health and in disposition: "I have a constitution in many respects peculiarly unhappy, attended with flaccid solids, vapid, sizy and scarce fluids; often occasioning a kind of childish weakness and contemptibleness of speech, presence and demeanor, with a disagreeable dullness and stiffness, much unfitting me for conversation, but more especially for the government of a college." He referred to his literary work: "My heart is so much in these studies which have long engaged and swallowed up my mind and been the chief entertainment and delight of my life, that I cannot find it in my heart to be willing to put myself into an incapacity to pursue them more in the future part of my life to such a degree as I must if I undertake to go through the same course of employ in the office of president that Mr. Burr did, instructing in all the languages and taking the whole care of the instruction of one of the classes, in all parts of learning, besides his other labors." "I think I can write better than I can speak," he added. He also mentioned his deficiency in algebra and the Greek classics. Such an extended list of objections is clear evidence that he did not want to give up his quiet life of scholarship. Yet he undeniably felt likewise the counter-attraction of the prestige of such an office as well as the opportunity to have a closer contact with the intellectual life of his generation, and to teach and preach to people who could think along with him. Otherwise he would hardly have concluded his letter with the assertion that in spite of his reluctance to accept he could not decline the invitation of so "worthy and venerable a body as that of the trustees of Nassau Hall" without seeking the advice of some of his "most wise friendly and faithful acquaintances"; nor would he have set forth a very specific interpretation of what would be his duties as president should he finally accept.

I should be willing to take upon me the work of a president, so far as it consists in the general inspection of the whole society; and to be subservient to the school as to their order and methods of study and instruction, assisting, myself, in the immediate instruction in the arts and sciences, (as discretion should direct, and occasion serve, and the state of things require,) especially of the senior class; and added to all, should be willing to do the whole work of a professor of divinity, in public and private lectures, proposing questions to be answered and some to be discussed in writing and free conversation, in meetings of graduates, and others appointed in proper seasons for these ends. It would be now out of my way to spend time in a constant teaching of the languages; unless it be the Hebrew tongue, which I should be willing to improve myself in by instructing others.

Among the members of the council which he called on January 4, 1758, were, of course, Bellamy and Hopkins. It seemed obvious to them that Edwards was just the man for the presidency. When they rendered their decision Edwards burst into tears, for he had not expected them to advise him to accept. Once the die was cast, however, and he had become reconciled to the new undertaking, he became quite composed and cheerful. He undertook the most terrific adjustment of his life with amazing speed and equanimity. Before the month was over he had preached his last sermon at the mission station on the text, "Here we have no continuing city" and left in triumph the town he had come to under a cloud seven years before. His good friend Samuel Hopkins preached the following Sunday, staying with Mrs. Edwards and the children, who, on account of the former's feeble health, were remaining in Stockbridge until the president's house should be ready for them.

Edwards' first month at Princeton was a busy one. He preached several times, selecting for his first discourse an old sermon, *The Unchangeableness of Christ*. So hurried had been the shift from pastorate to presidency he had not had time to prepare a new one. The very fact that he used an old sermon suggests that though externally he might have to alter considerably his habits and interests, he purposed to continue unchanged his old ways of thought and expression. He evidently still pictured himself as a pastor, charged with the care and cure of souls. That his people now were to be college boys instead of families made no essential difference to him.

He also held a number of theological discussions with the members of the senior class at which "they found so much entertainment and profit by it, especially by the light and instruction Mr. Edwards communicated in what he said upon the questions when they had delivered what they had to say, that they spoke of it with the greatest satisfaction and wonder."

He likewise attended a meeting of the board of trustees at which he was officially "fixed in the president's chair." It was evidently planned to postpone his inaugural address until the following commencement. This address, however, was destined never to be delivered, so that one can only conjecture what policies he would have enunciated in it. Undoubtedly he would have emphasized what he rightly believed to have been "the original and main design" of such an institution as Princeton, the training of men for the ministry. He would have included a declaration he had made when he was vainly trying to organize the revival of religion ten years before. As he had then written,

> I cannot but think that it is practicable enough so to constitute such societies that there should be no being there without being virtuous, serious, and diligent. It seems to me to be a reproach to the land that ever it should be so with our colleges, that instead of being places of the greatest advantages for true piety, one cannot send a child thither without great danger of his being infected as to his morals. . . . There is a great deal of pains taken to teach the scholars human learning; there ought to be as much, and more care, thoroughly to educate them in religion and lead them to true and eminent holiness. . . . It has been common in our public prayers to call these societies *the schools of the prophets*; and if they are schools to train up young men to be prophets, certainly there ought to be extraordinary care taken to train them up to be Christians. And I cannot see why it is not on all accounts fit and convenient for the governors and instructors of the colleges, particularly, singly and frequently to converse with the students about the state of their souls.

Richard C. Cabot once said that a course in ethics should do more than acquaint the student with a knowledge of ethical theory. It should make him a better man. Edwards would have wholeheartedly agreed. A college he defined as a "nursery of piety."

At this very time smallpox was epidemic in Princeton. Ever since its introduction by the

Spaniards in the later sixteenth century, smallpox had been one of the scourges of the New World. At the time Edwards was in college the wife of the English ambassador in Turkey, observing the beneficial results of inoculation as practiced by Greeks and Armenians, had had her own son inoculated. When, soon thereafter, the children of the Prince of Wales were similarly treated the new method became socially acceptable. Almost at once the death-rate dropped from one in five cases to one in three thousand. Yet both the disease and the prophylactic were still things of suspicion and dread. Edwards could recall the furore aroused in Boston in 1721 when, at the suggestion of the Reverend Cotton Mather, the native-born physician, Zabdiel Boylston, introduced the process in spite of the denunciations of the ministers and the protests of the only doctor there who was entitled to the degree. More recently the new president of Columbia had stipulated, before accepting the position, that whenever the disease became epidemic in New York he should be allowed to retire to Connecticut. And it was there as a matter of fact that he spent a large part of his time. Soon after his arrival in Princeton Edwards, having given the matter "the most deliberate and serious consultation," proposed to the trustees that he should be inoculated. As to why he should want to be —whether because of fear of the disease, or as an example to the community or to satisfy his scientific curiosity—unfortunately no record exists.

The inoculation appeared at first to have been

successful, but secondary complications set in and he became fatally ill. His daughter Lucy, who was living with Esther Burr, took care of him. Just what happened is not clear. According to the account of the attending physician, "although he had the smallpox favorably, yet having a number of them in the roof of his mouth and throat he could not possibly swallow a sufficient quantity of drink to keep off a secondary fever which proved too strong for his feeble frame." No word escaped him of rebellion that he had been uprooted in vain, that the strain of the last weeks of decision had gone for nothing or that the vistas of intellectual opportunity beckoned when he could not follow. Instead his dying thoughts were of the wife and children he loved so dearly and the God he loved so awesomely. "Dear Lucy," he said faintly to his daughter, "it seems to me to be the will of God that I must shortly leave you. Therefore give my kindest love to my dear wife and tell her that the uncommon union which has so long existed between us has been of such a nature as I trust is spiritual and therefore will continue forever; and I hope she will be supported under so great a trial and submit cheerfully to the will of God. And as to my children, you are now like to be left fatherless; which I hope will be an inducement to you all to seek a Father who will never fail you."

"As to my funeral," he concluded, his habit of philanthropy asserting itself, "I would have it to be simply decent, like Mr. Burr's; and any additional money that might be expected to be laid out that way I would have it disposed of to charitable uses. . . . Trust in God and ye shall not fear," were his last words.

Jonathan Edwards had been in Princeton only two months when, on March 22, 1758, at the height of his career, he died. As if his own death were not tragedy enough, three weeks later his recently widowed daughter Esther died—apparently likewise of complications resulting from the anti-smallpox inoculation. Six months later Mrs. Edwards, too, was dead. Father and mother, daughter and son-in-law, dying almost within the year, lie buried side by side in Princeton.

Though Edwards was cut off in the fullness of his power, his life does not suggest incompleteness. It rounded into a perfect whole because it had a fixed and single center. That burning core of conviction had flashed upon him in his youth, an intuition of God as a Being who was to him at once majestic and holy, beautiful and loving, and in comparison with whom everything else in the world of nature and of man was as nothing. To the intellectual and emotional implications of that haunting vision he devoted his life with all the intensity of his ardent nature, disciplining mind and body in its behalf. It conditioned the solution of every problem that presented itself to his vigorous and restless mind. Fascinated as he was by the operations of the human spirit, he could view them only in their relation to the ultimate Reality. That is why he thought of people and dealt with them in terms of their rebellion, their self-deception, and their aspiration for the life abundant, their inner conflicts, and their specious contentment with less than the best. In the vast field of cosmological speculation where almost alone of his generation he found himself at ease he finally rejected every interpretation which failed to do justice to his intuition of personality and activity as the fundamental features of reality. Into his reflections on the sanctions and objectives of the good life he introduced his religious reference. Even his passing glimpses of beauty he grounded in the very being of God. Political theory and practice, economics, general science, business, the arts—with the exception of education—he left untouched. Yet indirectly he affected the culture of the American colonies by his impressive contribution to the revival of religion both through his writings and through the impact of his spirit upon the lives of numberless men and women.

Above all others of his own time he made a name for America at home and overseas. He still maintains his position as one of the most stimulating and forceful minds America has produced.

Acknowledgments

For placing source material at my disposal and for other assistance I am gratefully indebted to several librarians and to members of their staffs, notably: Dr. James Thayer Gerould, Princeton University Library; Dr. William W. Rockwell, Union Theological Seminary Library; Dr. Owen Hamilton Gates, Andover-Harvard Library; Dr. Matthew Spinka, Hammond Library, The Chicago Theological Seminary; J. L. Harrison, Esq., Forbes Library, Northampton, Massachusetts; Dr. Andrew Keogh, Yale University Library. By the last named I have been given permission to quote from the Journal of Esther Burr and from Edwards' so-called "Catalogue of Books," both of which manuscripts are in the Yale Library.

By the counsel and criticisms of the discriminating editor of this series, as well as of several of my colleagues and students and of various members of my family, I have greatly profited. I should like to add this formal acknowledgment of my appreciation to the thanks I have already privately expressed to them.

A. C. M., Jr.

Chicago

Books to Consult

1. By Edwards

The Works of Jonathan Edwards. Worcester, 1808.
 This edition, which has been many times reprinted, in four volumes, contains all of Edwards' important published writings.

The Works of Jonathan Edwards. New York, 1829.
 Though no single complete collection of Edwards' writings exists, this ten-volume edition is far and away the most inclusive. The first volume contains the indispensable *Memoirs* by Dr. S. E. Dwight.

Christian Love. Edited by Tryon Edwards. 1851.

Selections from the Unpublished Writings of Jonathan Edwards, Edited by Alexander B. Grosart, 1865.

An Unpublished Essay of Edwards on the Trinity, by George P. Fisher. New York, 1903.

Jonathan Edwards' "Catalogue of Books" by James A. Caskey, 1931.
 This valuable transcript and interpretation is in the Hammond Library of the Chicago Theological Seminary, in the form of a typewritten manuscript.

A complete list of the editions and reprints of Edwards' collected and individual works is being prepared by James Thayer Gerould, Librarian of Princeton University.

2. About Edwards

Jonathan Edwards, by A. V. G. Allen. Boston, Houghton Mifflin Company, 1890.

> The standard treatment; mainly theological in emphasis with less attention to Edwards' psychological and æsthetic interests and to his personal life.

Jonathan Edwards, The Fiery Puritan, by Henry Bamford Parkes. New York, Minton Balch, 1930.

> Useful for the light it throws on contemporary manners and customs rather than for its understanding of Edwards' own thinking. It contains important bibliographical references.

The Puritan Mind, by Herbert Wallace Schneider. New York, Henry Holt & Company, Inc., 1930.

> One of the best chapters of the book deals with Edwards. The admirable bibliography includes both source material and all the important general books, such as Foster's *History of New England Theology*.

The Story of Religions in America, by William Warren Sweet. New York, Harper & Brothers, 1931.

> The only volume of its kind on the subject. Prof. Sweet is interested more in the spread of Christianity than in its theological development and expression.

Piety Versus Morality, the Passing of the New England Theology, by Joseph Haroutunian. New York, Henry Holt & Company, Inc., 1932.

The Dictionary of American Biography contains an illuminating and extraordinarily compact account of Edwards by Francis A. Christie.

The Cambridge History of American Literature has a brief but delightful article by Paul Elmore More.

"The Radicalism of Jonathan Edwards," by Frederic Ives Carpenter, *The New England Quarterly*, October, 1931, presents an aspect of Edwards' mind that deserves emphasis.

Chronology

1. EARLY YEARS

1701 Yale founded
1703 Jonathan Edwards (and John Wesley) born
1720 Graduated from Yale
1724 Tutor at Yale

2. NORTHAMPTON

1727 Ordained at Northampton
1731 *God Glorified in Man's Dependence*, Edwards' first published sermon
1735 Revival of religion at Northampton
1736 *Narrative of Surprising Conversions*
1739 George Whitefield's second visit to America
1740-42 The Great Awakening
1741 *Distinguishing Marks of a Work of the Spirit of God*
1742 *Some Thoughts Concerning the Present Revival of Religion in New England*
1746 Princeton founded
1746 *Treatise Concerning the Religious Affections*
1749 *Memoirs of David Brainerd*
1749 Qualifications for Full Communion
1750 Edwards dismissed from Northampton Church

3. STOCKBRIDGE

1751 Edwards goes to Stockbridge
1754 *Freedom of the Will*
1755-63 Seven Years War: England and France competing for America and India
1755 *Dissertation Concerning the End for Which God Created the World, and Dissertation on the Nature of True Virtue*
1756 Aaron Burr, Edwards' grandson, born
1758 *Original Sin*

4. PRINCETON

1758 Edwards installed as President of Princeton (February 16)
1758 Edwards died (March 22)
1764 Samuel Hopkins published Edwards' *Memoirs*

Index

Adams, Charles Francis, 116
Addison, 101
Æsthetics, 16, 175f., 178ff., 188ff.
Amyrault, 158
Arminianism, 34, 52, 128, 152, 154ff., 161f., 173

Barth, Karl, 174
Beauty, 16, 30, 40, 78f., 81, 83, 175f., 178f., 188ff., 197, 199, 214
Belcher, Governor, 202, 205
Bellamy, Joseph, 92, 153, 167ff., 208
Berkeley, George, 21f.
Bible, 7, 25, 29, 42, 59, 67, 80, 87, 103, 113f., 120, 156, 172, 185, 197, 201
  authority of, 25, 80, 87, 114, 120, 156, 172, 185, 197
Boylston, Zabdiel, 211
Brainerd, David, 104ff., 141ff., 150, 152
Breck, Robert, 51, 125
Bundling, 115f.
Burr, Aaron, 147, 202f., 205, 207, 212f.
Burr, Esther Edwards, 147, 203ff., 212f.

Cabot, Richard C., 210
Calvinism, 27, 29, 33f., 39, 51f., 154ff., 159, 171ff., 183, 185
Carlyle, Thomas, 40f.

Church of England, 6, 33f., 96
Church membership, 118f., 122, 132
Colden, Cadwallader, 18
Coleridge, 40
Columbia (King's College), 5, 211
Congregationalism, 33f., 66, 130f.
Cromwell, Oliver, 86
Cudworth, Ralph, 21f., 187f.

Disinterestedness, 79, 81, 84f., 107, 197, 199

Education, 2f., 60, 66, 148ff., 214
Edwards, Jerusha, 104ff.
Edwards, Jonathan, writings of:
  Brainerd's Memoirs, 105ff.
  Christian Love, 59
  College notes, 9ff., 175, 180, 184, 187, 189ff.
  Distinguishing Marks of a Work of the Spirit, 62f.
  End for Which God Created the World, 170ff., 175, 183, 188
  Freedom of the Will, 152ff., 160ff.
  History of Work of Redemption, 59, 201f.
  Narrative of Surprising Conversions, 37, 49f., 53ff., 62, 120

223

Edwards, Jonathan—(*Continued*)
- *Nature of True Virtue*, 188ff.
- *Original Sin*, 156, 160
- *Religious Affections*, 68f., 73ff., 80, 83, 87, 104, 106, 121
- sermons, 39, 42f., 53, 59, 69, 81, 83f., 90, 94, 98f., 112ff., 136f., 201f., 209
- *Some Thoughts Concerning the Present Revival*, 63
- *Treatise on Grace*, 75
- *Unchangeableness of Christ* (sermon), 209
- *Union in Prayer*, 102

Edwards, Sarah Pierrepont, Mrs., 37ff., 61, 71f., 91ff., 121ff., 139, 167f., 204, 208, 212f.
Edwards, Timothy, 1f., 7, 26, 48f., 97
Edwards, Mrs. Timothy, 2f., 27
Emerson, Ralph Waldo, 22, 157, 164, 182f.
Emmons, Nathanael, 153
England, 9, 33, 63ff., 86, 186
Erskine, John, 153, 169
Ethics, 7, 23f., 75, 78, 81, 86f., 187ff., 196ff., 214
Evangelicalism, 40

Fabre, Jean Henri, 15
Franklin, Benjamin, 6, 18, 100, 205

Great Awakening, 40, 59ff., 64, 67, 78, 112, 122f., 140, 168

Half-Way Covenant, 118f.
Hampshire County Ministers Association, 95f., 102, 121

Harvard, 1f., 7, 51, 101
Hawley, Joseph, 128f.
Hell, 43, 83
Hellenism, 159, 167, 188, 192, 194
Hobbes, Thomas, 164, 196
Hocking, W. E., 19
Hopkins, Samuel, 91f., 153, 167ff., 175, 199, 208
Hume, David, 187
Hutcheson, Francis, 187f., 193, 196
Hutchinson, Anne, 86

Inge, Dean, 188
Intuition, 85ff., 193
Irenæus, 166

James, William, 68f., 75
Johnson, James Weldon, 165
Johnson, Samuel, 5ff., 21, 33f., 211

Keats, 188

Liberalism, religious, 173f.
Lippmann, Walter, 27
Locke, John, 7f., 21, 86
Lord's Supper, 119f.
Love, 75f., 78f., 81ff., 175f., 194ff.

Mather, Cotton, 211
Milton, 101
Missions, 22, 60, 104ff., 139ff., 149f.
Montanists, 86
Muir, John, 15
Mysticism, 30, 86ff.

Newton, Sir Isaac, 8, 16, 18, 100

Pantheism, 180ff.
Pepperell, Sir William, 145, 148

INDEX

Perfection, 76, 109, 111f., 179
Philosophy, 19ff., 34
Pietism, 40ff.
Plato, 21, 188, 194
Pope, Alexander, 101
Presbyterianism, 32, 66
Princeton, 108, 153, 202ff.
Psychology, 8, 11, 56, 67ff., 172

Quakers, 33, 86

Revival of Religion, 40, 62, 65f., 69f., 107, 120, 155
Revival of 1734-35, 40ff.
Revival of 1740-42. *See* Great Awakening
Richardson, Samuel, 101, 117
Roman Catholicism, 96, 103
Romanticism, 30, 40, 178
Rousseau, 40
Royal Society, 18

Schleiermacher, 40
Science, 7, 14ff., 23, 34, 56, 68, 100, 185
Scotland, 102f., 126, 130, 151, 153, 169, 186f., 203
Self-love, 82ff., 184, 196ff.
Sergeant, John, 168

Shaftesbury, third Earl of, 7, 187f., 196
Society in London for Propogating the Gospel in New England, 145f.
Steele, Sir Richard, 100
Stephen, Leslie, 116
Stoddard, Col. John, 97, 124ff., 140
Stoddard, Solomon, 2, 35, 39f., 48, 50, 119ff., 126ff.
Stoicism, 27, 29

Twain, Mark, 111

Watts, Isaac, 49, 101
Wesley, John, 63, 101
Westminster Catechism, 7, 81, 150
Whitby, Daniel, 152
Whitefield, George, 60f., 167
Williams, Elisha, 5f., 34f., 145
Williams, Ephraim, 144ff.
Williams, Israel, 53, 125f., 132
Wollaston, Thomas, 184, 187
Woodbridge, Timothy, 144
Wordsworth, 41

Yale, 4ff., 32ff., 37, 62, 70, 95, 101, 104, 140, 153, 167, 203, 206